Books by Douglas J. Wood

Fiction

Presidential Intentions
Presidential Declarations
Presidential Conclusions
Dark Data: Control, Alt, Delete
Dragon on the Far Side of the Moon
Blood on the Bayou
The Shakespeare Killer

Non-Fiction

Please be Ad-Vised
101 Things I Want to Say
Asshole Attorney

from dawn to dusk

from dawn to dusk

How to Build a Multimillion Dollar Law Practice and Then Give it Away

Douglas J. Wood

Copyright © 2024 by Douglas J. Wood

All rights reserved. no part of this publication may be reproduced, distributed, or transmitted in any form or by any means, including photocopying, recording, or other electronic or mechanical methods, without the prior written permission of the publisher except in the case of brief quotations embodied in critical reviews and certain other noncommercial uses permitted by copyright law.

For permission requests, contact the publisher at the website below:

Plum Bay Publishing, LLC
www.plumbaypublishing.com

Library of Congress Control Number: 2024905656

Paperback ISBN: 979-8-9858564-6-0
Hardcover ISBN: 979-8-9858564-9-1
eBook ISBN: 979-8-9858564-8-4
Printed in the United States of America

Cover Design: Tanja Prokop

Interior Design: Tracy Atkins

Editors: Jeremy Townsend, Carol Bernstein, and Nancy Schulein

To every mentor I've had, a list that could fill pages.

Contents

Preamble..1
   Why Should You Listen to Me? 2
PART ONE: DAWN..7
Establishing a Written Plan 9
   Step One—A SWOT Analysis. 9
   Step Two—Setting Strategic Goals.......................................9
   Step Three—Tactics..16
   Step Four—Reviewing the Plan 17
   Step Five—Revising the Plan 17
   Step Six—Grading Your Performance................................17
   Step Seven—Doing It All Again 18
Tips and Tricks..19
Part Two: Dusk 53
Embracing Irrelevancy 55
The Reality of Irrelevancy 56
Rude Awakening 58
Moving On..62
Planning..65
Mapping Success 67
Taking Steps...70
Attitude 72
Emotional Challenges..74
External Stress 76
Internal Stress 79
Trust..81
Loyalty 83
Disappointment..85
Anger...87
Humor 90
Jerks..92
Diversions 95
The End of Adding Value 97
Respect..100
Leadership 102

Transparency	104
A Lesson Not Learned	108
Relaxing	110
Do Not Do List	112
Improvement	113
What is Good for the Goose . .	117
Support	119
The Bottom Line	121
The Final Word	122
Appendix A:	124
Step One	124
Step Two	128
Step Three	128
Steps Four	130
Step Five	131
Step Six	132
Step Seven	132
Appendix B	133
Jeffrey Lant Seven Contact Matrix	133
Appendix C	134
Tactics	134
Appendix D	138
Picking Mentors	138
Appendix E	140
Understanding Your Numbers	140
Appendix F	144
Maintaining Your Reputation	144
Promotion Bingo	147
Appendix H	149
Transition Program Ideas	149
Appendix I	153
Recommended Reading	153
Acknowledgments	154

Preamble

This book takes readers through the life cycle of a successful lawyer, from building a multimillion practice (Dawn) to passing on a practice and winding down as retirement approaches (Dusk).

The principles are based on longstanding business practices that are, unfortunately, rarely followed by lawyers. So, while the teachings are helpful in any business venture, they're tailored particularly to lawyers. Those who can put their egos aside and accept that concepts taught in business school can apply to developing a legal practice and maneuvering to retirement when the time comes will hopefully find ideas to guide their future, both at the beginning and near the end.

Dawn—Part One of the book—covers the process of business planning and how to systematically approach growing a successful legal practice. While countless books have been written on building a business and some focused on legal practices, this book provides proven actionable steps anyone can take to ensure success. Building a large practice is uncomfortable for some lawyers. Most lack the skills to succeed. Those skills, however, can be learned. So, if building a practice is your goal, this book will tell you how.

Dusk—Part Two of the book—provides guidance on how to deal with winding down a practice from both a business and emotional perspective. Unlike Part One, Part Two is inevitable for every lawyer. You have a choice whether you want to build a practice. Eventually, however, every lawyer has to end his or her career. Sometimes pleasantly, sometimes traumatically. This book helps lawyers who have reached that stage in their careers take control of the process and avoid letting others dictate their destiny.

While both Parts reflect my professional experience during an over forty-seven-year career, Dusk is particularly personal, discussing the challenges I faced in transitioning my practice. I hope readers will apply what I experienced to their own journey.

Each part has some sections that resemble one another and may seem redundant. That is intentional. Dawn is for younger lawyers building a practice. Dusk is for lawyers who are approaching the end of their careers. Many of the principles I discuss apply to both. Hence, some of the redundancy. While the better approach is to read the entire book, if you're not in the demographic that Part One or Part Two addresses, each can be read independently.

Not every piece of advice will apply to you. But much of it will. Some advice is based on my experience that might not directly apply to you. Likewise, some of what you read will seem obvious. When you believe something is irrelevant to you or is obvious, ask yourself what part might be relevant and whether you act on those things you see as obvious. Or when you've seen them, do you say to yourself, "Damn, I should have thought of that!" Business writer Harvey Mackay calls it "The blinding glimpse of the obvious." It's always been in front of you, but you didn't see it. You only realized it when someone else saw it and won the business. Often, looking at the obvious contributes as much to success as revelations. I'll test your powers of observation later in this book.

The book also includes an extensive Appendix that supports the advice and offers forms, worksheets, and additional ideas to assist in your development and transition.

Why Should You Listen to Me?

You should ask yourself, Why should I listen to him? Sure, I might have had a successful career, built a multi-million-dollar practice, and then transitioned it to others, but what makes me an expert in helping you build or transition your law practice?

Perhaps a brief history of my career will give you reason to consider my advice worthy of your time.

While it may sound like a cliché (because it is), I had nothing going for me when I pursued a legal career. My record in undergraduate school was mediocre. Some might say I majored in college parties and did not pay adequate attention to my studies. As graduation with a degree in political science approached, the prospect of getting a decent job seemed doubtful, so I took the LSAT. I did very well. With confidence that my high score would overcome my disappointing GPA, I applied to twelve top one hundred law schools, all of which rejected me. So, I finished college and took a job as an adjuster for Liberty Mutual Insurance Company. After six months of investigating slip and falls and fender benders, Liberty promoted me to a trial adjuster accompanying lawyers to court. While I enjoyed the work, it wasn't what I wanted to do, so I tried the law school route again, applying to thirteen law schools, all different from the prior year's list. Eventually, all but one rejected me—the newly founded Franklin Pierce Law Center in Concord, New Hampshire. But one out of twenty-five was all I needed! When I entered what became the school's first class, it had provisional ABA accreditation. For the first two years, we literally had our classes in a refurbished barn of a former bull breeding operation. Our professors were a mixed lot. As one put it, he came to teach in New Hampshire to get out of the pollution of New York City and to see leaves in the fall.

~~asshole~~ attorney

MUSINGS, MEMORIES, AND ~~missteps~~ missteps IN A 40 YEAR CAREER

Douglas J. Wood

Once I started law school, I finally put my nose to the grindstone and worked hard, knowing I never wanted to return to insurance. I graduated at the top of my class. But there were no decent jobs for graduates from an unknown law school. So, I went to New York University and got an LLM in Trade Regulation (essentially consumer protection and intellectual property law). One afternoon between classes, I noticed an index card on the wall of the placement office for a small firm looking for a part-time clerk. I interviewed and got the job. The firm was Abeles Clark & Osterberg, a well-known entertainment litigation boutique. I had no idea at the time how famous they were and how lucky I was to get the job. They eventually hired me as an associate. It was the ultimate music business job. I literally hung out with rock stars and TV personalities, hopping from club to club in the heyday of the NYC Greenwich Village scene—CBGB's, the Bottom Line, Purple Onion, and Bitter End. A year into the gig, I realized I would not survive. I remember telling my wife that I had to get out before I became an alcoholic or drug addict or both hanging out with glitterati. The glamor of the job was fading quickly. So, I sent my résumé to every NYC intellectual property law firm listed in Martindale-Hubbell (then the only source for law firm listings). I got hired by Hall, Dickler, Lawler, Kent & Howley, a firm known for its entertainment work. But I wasn't hired because of my experience or class record. The firm interviewed me only because I'd done a clerkship with the Army's JAG Corp in Wurzburg, Germany, between my second and third year of law school. The senior partner hired me because he was stationed in Wurzburg after WWII and liked to talk about it. That's not a joke.

So, I started with no business, no significant contacts, and a JD from an unknown law school. While the LLM from NYU helped, I was hardly sought after. But, as the saying goes, the rest is history.

I never inherited a single client over the years I was at Hall Dickler. I had great mentors, but they never gave clients to anyone. That's just the way it was back then. So, one day, I figured out how to build my own business book. I read many business books and talked to successful folks I knew. Then, in or about 1980, I started writing business plans. I got better every year. Today, my yearly plans are over fifty pages. I live by them.

I eventually took over the operation of Hall Dickler and, in 2004, merged most of the firm into Reed Smith, a law firm with over 1700 lawyers—what is often called "Big Law." Over the next twenty years, I continued to build my practice and became one of the firm's top producers with an eight-figure book of business. I established and ran the firm's entertainment and media law practice group. I served on the Executive Committee. I was the managing partner of the New York office. Part One of this Book—Dawn—takes you through my journey and suggests how you can have the same success.

But time waits for no one.

In 2018, I realized I'd automatically cease to be an equity partner on December 31, 2020. It was always in the partnership agreement, but I didn't notice it in 2004. Now, it was reality.

Consistent with my commitment to business planning, I developed a plan to transition my practice, working with the firm to execute it. So, on January 1, 2021, I became Senior Counsel and, under my agreement with the firm, began a rigorous transition of passing my practice to others. I completed the transition by the end of 2023. I passed millions of dollars' worth of clients to others under a specific plan. Everyone was a winner.

On January 1, 2024, I left Reed Smith and started my solo practice—not to work full time but to keep myself active by helping a few select clients and continuing a pursuit I've enjoyed—mentoring junior attorneys on building their business. Having experienced the end of an attorney's professional journey, I also mentored senior attorneys approaching retirement. From "Dawn to Dusk." Part Two of this Book—Dusk—takes you through the end of my career in Big Law and the success I enjoyed in planning and executing the transition.

I attribute the millions of dollars I brought into Hall Dickler and Reed Smith in the last forty years and the rewards I received in transitioning it all to others—and the many millions I earned—to one thing: planning.

If you want to learn more about my journey, you can read it in my memoirs, *Asshole Attorney: Musings, Memories, and Missteps in a 40 Year Career*. It's available on Amazon, Barnes & Noble and other bookstores. It won the 2019 Independent Press Award for best humor and wit. So, reading it might at least make you laugh.

The point is, if I could do it, you can, too. All you need to do is have a plan. This book provides a roadmap to establish a profitable practice and exit on your terms.

PART ONE: DAWN

Establishing a Written Plan

With rare exceptions, every accomplished businessperson will tell you that planning is essential to achieving success. Unlike luck or having a client passed down to you (gifts you should welcome), a written plan is the best roadmap to success. But it needs to be based on time-proven methodologies, not by the seat of the pants. It must be carefully considered, written down, reviewed, and revised. Goals must be based upon your abilities and be attainable. While reaching high is okay, establishing goals that are realistically out of reach will only frustrate you and reduce your likelihood of success.

The planning process I take you through is well-established and based on principles taught in every business school. Unfortunately, such things are not taught in law school. It includes seven steps:

Step One—A SWOT Analysis.

You must do an honest assessment of yourself. That is most easily done through a SWOT analysis that lists your strengths, weaknesses, opportunities, and threats. SWOT is an approach taught in every business school and adopted by virtually every successful business. But it's rarely adopted by individuals. That's a pity. It works at every level. But to work, you must be brutally honest and objective. Appendix A has a form you can use.

Step Two—Setting Strategic Goals.

Establish specific goals you wish to accomplish in the coming year. Use the results of your SWOT analysis to help you establish them. For example, what goals will your strengths support? What can you do to address your weaknesses? What opportunities can be translated into goals? What strategy can you undertake to thwart your threats? Keep in mind that these are strategic, not tactical. The goal is what you want to achieve, not how you will do it.

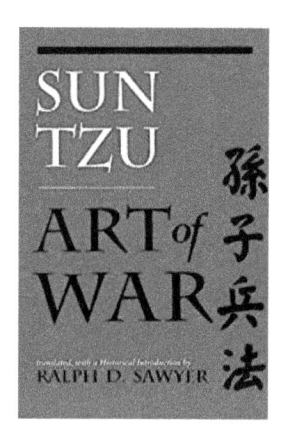

The difference between strategy and tactics is often confusing. Sun Tzu's *The Art of War*, described as the oldest military treatise in the world, may help you understand the importance of both strategic goals and specific tactics. According to Sun Tzu, strategy is about winning before the battle begins, while tactics are about striking weaknesses. Put another way, strategy is an overarching plan or set of goals. Changing strategies is like turning around an aircraft carrier—it can be done, but not quickly. Tactics are the specific actions or steps you undertake to accomplish your strategy that you can change as circumstances dictate. But any change must always stay true to the goal.

For lawyers, strategic goals in your personal business plan should NOT be billable hours, utilization rates (the percentage of your billable hours to the minimum established by the firm), realization (the percentage of revenue received vs. amount billed), or working attorney receipts (WAR—the revenue collected on your billable hours). Shocking? Not really. Billable hours, utilization, realization, and WAR are goals set for you by your firm. While you should strive to accomplish those goals, the goals in your plan are what you want to achieve for yourself that will make you a better lawyer and business producer. Clients couldn't care less about the statistics that measure your firm's performance. They care about your ability to help improve their performance. Delivering on those expectations is at the core of business planning.

Examples of strategic goals that might be personal to you include:

- Increase my direct acquisition of clients by [x]%.
- Increase my work for existing clients by [x]%.
- Improve my relationship with [insert name, e.g., a senior partner or General Counsel at a client].
- Strengthen my relationship with [insert client].
- Delegate work to others in the firm.
- Increase my public profile.
- Raise myself in lawyer rankings, e.g., *Chambers* or the *Legal 500*.
- Get published.

You may have a completely unique set of strategic goals depending upon your SWOT analysis, politics at your firm, the number of years you've practiced, your specialty, etc. There is no perfect list, but any list is better than none.

Let me expand on three strategic goals I gave myself over the years:

Goal One: Increase my direct acquisition of clients—This is the direct measure of your "book." These are the clients you bring in. Setting a goal of increasing that statistic is personal and appropriate in an individual plan.

Goal Two: Increase work for existing clients—This is a critical measure many firms use to evaluate your performance by seeing how well you work with existing clients. This is measured differently from firm to firm. Some firms follow this by allocating income credits from a client to those attorneys who work on a matter. This allocation usually occurs when a matter first comes in (although the allocation can be changed later if circumstances change, e.g., a new attorney takes up the bulk of the work).

The higher your interaction with a particular client, the more you have integrated yourself and increased the likelihood that you may eventually control the client as transitions occur. The more you delegate work to others, the faster those clients grow. The more you're willing to work on clients you didn't originate, the better you'll be respected by your peers. All of that will hit the bottom line of your compensation and insure your future.

Here's one example from a firm that allocates credits in three columns:

Client Relationship Attorney (CRA)—This is the attorney who brings in the client. The Big Kahuna. At some firms, it's also called client originations. The originating attorney gets credit in the CRA column for 100 percent of the fees regardless of who does the work. CRA should be your long-term focus to get to the top of the heap. More on how to do that later.

Matter Originating Attorney (MOA)—Where an attorney brings in a new matter for a client when he or she is not the CRA, they are allocated a percentage of the total revenue received to their MOA bucket. The percentage is often negotiated between the CRA and the attorney seeking MOA since more than one attorney might bring in a matter, including the CRA.

Matter Responsible Attorney (MRA)—This bucket covers attorneys who originate neither the client nor the matter but who manage the matter, in whole or in part. This is also a negotiated percentage of the revenue received, since more than one attorney may have responsibility for running a matter.

Here's what this allocation method looks like on a spreadsheet, using two examples—one that is generous and builds teamwork and one that is greedy and reflects a poor partner:

Client: Amalgamated Enterprises					
CRA: Jane Doe					
Matter: Initial Public Offering					
Fees Received:	$1,000,000				
Allocations:					
	CRA	**MOA**	**MRA**		
Jane Doe	100%	25%	10%		
John Doe	0%	50%	25%		
Bill Bloggs	0%	25%	25%		
Sally Bloggs	0%	0%	40%		
$ Credits:				**Total**	% of Credits
Jane Doe	$1,000,000	$250,000	$100,000	$1,350,000	45%
John Doe	$0	$500,000	$250,000	$750,000	25%
Bill Bloggs	$0	$250,000	$250,000	$500,000	17%
Sally Bloggs	$0	$0	$400,000	$400,000	13%
Total:	$1,000,000	$1,000,000	$1,000,000	$3,000,000	

In this example, Jane Doe brought in the client and gets 100 percent of the revenue credits for all matters. She acknowledges the contribution of John Doe and Bill Bloggs in bringing in the matter with some MOA. Finally, she gives credit to Sally Bloggs because she will run the matter.

Contrast this with a greedy CRA who is not generous with MOA and MRA. A spreadsheet for a greedy CRA might look like this:

Establishing a Written Plan

Client: Amalgamated Enterprises					
CRA: Jane Doe					
Matter: Initial Public Offering					
Fees Received:	$1,000,000				
Allocations:					
	CRA	MOA	MRA		
Jane Doe	100%	80%	60%		
John Doe	0%	10%	0%		
Bill Bloggs	0%	10%	0%		
Sally Bloggs	0%	0%	40%		
$ Credits:				Total	% of Credits
Jane Doe	$1,000,000	$800,000	$600,000	$2,400,000	80%
John Doe	$0	$100,000	$0	$100,000	3%
Bill Bloggs	$0	$100,000	$0	$100,000	3%
Sally Bloggs	$0	$0	$400,000	$400,000	13%
Total:	$1,000,000	$1,000,000	$1,000,000	$3,000,000	

What do these contrasting spreadsheets tell Jane's firm and her colleagues?

The first one shows a partner who is building a team. The second one illustrates someone who does not like to cede control or autonomy to her colleagues. She is not institutionalizing the client. She is unlikely to garner loyalty from her colleagues to work on her matters when the credits they receive are unfairly low.

Thus, if a CRA doles out a lot of MOA and MRA and also has MOA and MRA for clients that are not his or her originations, that shows a real team player. While these numbers can seem arbitrary, in sum they tell an authentic story.

Obviously, in my example, it looks as though every dollar is tripled. If we could do that, we'd all be rich. Instead, by seeing how the splits compare from a percentage perspective, the system allows management to get a picture of the CRA's performance on team building and each attorney's contribution to the firm's success. It can all be used to determine how CRA, MOA, and MRA impact an individual's compensation.

If you're not at the point of your career where you can originate clients and get a lot of CRA, your best bet is to push for as much MOA and MRA as you can when work comes your way and try to work for partners who are generous in their allocations. Your road to success may be much longer if they are not.

That's just one example. There are others. Just be sure you know the credit methodology used by your firm. You can't exploit it if you don't understand it.

Goal Three: Decrease my unbilled time and accounts receivable. Billing is the lifeblood of a law firm. The faster a firm gets its bills out, the sooner collections occur. The more a firm empowers its businesspeople rather than its attorneys to deal with the billing and collections process, the better the firm will do. Business professionals know what they're doing. Trust them and get out of their way. Throughout my career, I rarely looked at a bill before it went out. I trusted my assistant and others to get bills out professionally and promptly. When I suggest that approach to others, many react that they can't imagine not reviewing an invoice before it is sent to a client, making sure the time is appropriate, and determining if something needs to be written off. Ethical rules require that you ensure your fees are reasonable. But you're not the only one who can do so. Those reluctant to depend upon professionals fear clients will get angry with billing they don't review. Perhaps they're right. But following my approach for over forty-five years has never cost me a client. Whenever they objected to a bill, we discussed and adjusted it when appropriate.

Another word to the wise on billing. Writing off time before you bill it is the equivalent of giving your work away for free. That is not a sustainable business model. And not collecting on fees you have billed is worse. While I do not deny that sometimes a write-off is warranted, they are few and far between. Over the years, I've heard every conceivable excuse from attorneys: so and so put in too much time, the client will never pay it, the results were bad, etc., etc. And I've heard every excuse from clients: I didn't expect it to cost so much, I didn't budget for it, I'm a little short on money right now, etc. etc. More often than not, I don't buy it. I trust my colleagues, bill the time they record, and let the client react. Then, decide if a write-off is warranted. I never lost a client over billing. If you disagree with my philosophy, that's fine. Remember that you're decreasing your book and delaying

Establishing a Written Plan

your advancement the next time you write off pre-billing or post-billing. It is literally money out of your pocket. Good luck with that. Jack Warner, a client who owned a successful advertising agency, used to say that if a client doesn't pay you, it's stealing from you.

Conversely, you're stealing from a colleague if you write off his or her time without legitimate reasons. And you're stealing from your firm. No one wants to deal with someone who steals.

Regardless, it's critical that you fully understand your "numbers" and how your firm calculates them. Appendix E provides a deeper analysis.

Step Three—Tactics.

Establish specific tactics you plan to use to accomplish each of your goals. Tactics address the questions:

- What are you going to do?
- When are you going to do it?
- How are you going to do it?
- Who do you need to help you execute the tactic?
- Why will your tactic help you achieve the goal?

Each goal should have multiple tactics. For example, suppose your goal is to increase work from a particular client. In that case, tactics might include entertaining the CEO, CFO, or GC, delivering a training session of interest to the client, inviting key people to firm events, etc. The more numerous and specific the tactics, the easier they are to schedule and accomplish. The more tactics you adopt and details you provide on the What, When, How, Who, and Why, the more likely you will achieve the goal.

By comparison, a tactic listed as "Get to know the GC better" is misplaced. That is not a tactic. It lacks specific steps you will take to get to know the GC better. "Get to know the GC better" is more of a goal. You must understand the difference.

Entrepreneur Michael Blumberg once wrote, "Enhance your skills, put in the time, and make tactical plans for the next few steps. Then, based on what happens, look one more move ahead and adjust the plans." The key to his advice is the need for a plan and flexible supporting tactics. A plan alone is only an idea. The tactics bring it to life.

Further ideas for tactics are provided in Appendix C.

Step Four—Reviewing the Plan

Create a schedule when you will review and update the plan. If you have someone who can help you, e.g., your assistant, all the better. You must periodically review the plan and not just leave it in your desk drawer. The review should occur at least once a month. Put reminders in your calendar. Without religiously following this step, you will fail. I cannot stress that enough.

Step Five—Revising the Plan

Revise the plan as the year progresses. As the saying goes, the plan is a "living document" and is not etched in stone. Things and circumstances change, and adjustments must be made. For example, if the underlying basis for a goal becomes moot, drop it. That might happen if the target merges with another company or your contacts leave. The plan might also be revised if your efforts are failing. The lesson is not to chase windmills. If someone you've targeted is not responding after many attempts, drop them as a goal or tactic and add someone or something else. Here's a tip: if you have a large screen for your computer, always keep your business plan open. That will cause you to look at it when you have a break. It's that simple.

Step Six—Grading Your Performance

At year's end, grade yourself by noting how many of the tactics you executed and the goals you accomplished.

Establishing a Written Plan

Step Seven—Doing It All Again

Update your SWOT analysis. Then, adopt a new plan for the following year.

Taking these seven steps consistently year after year will guarantee you succeed. The key is to stay diligent, remain patient, and understand that some things you try won't work. Don't be discouraged. As Winston Churchill said, "Success is the ability to go from failure to failure without losing your enthusiasm."

Tips and Tricks

In building a multi-million-dollar book of business, I've come to realize that besides the basics, there are many common tactics in business development, whether it's building a law practice or selling widgets. I've researched some for better understanding and simply accepted others on their face. I've used them all. They all served me well. Here are some I hope will help you.

They are tactical. Perhaps they'll help you develop your own tactics.

Fundamentals. As in any endeavor, adhering to fundamentals is essential to success. We see this most often in athletics. If you speak to any elite athlete, he or she will tell you that staying true to the fundamentals of a sport best assures victory. They practice them daily, whether shooting baskets or driving golf balls. In each instance, they break it down. What should the arc be on a basketball shot? How is it best to hit a wedge to a green or make a tricky putt? They teach themselves the fundamentals through repetition and gain muscle memory. With lawyers, it's mental memory that applies. So, remembering the fundamentals of the law and business disciplines must be mastered. Much of what I describe are examples of those fundamentals.

Put it in writing. Every business school teaches its MBA candidates that success is contingent on planning. They also teach that plans must be in writing. That's pretty simple. We covered that in the previous "Seven Steps to Success." But there is more to it than professorial oratory. Putting things in writing and keeping them in eyesight has both psychological and physiological effects that help ensure you will accomplish the tasks at hand.

Supporting this are two concepts described as "external storage" and "encoding." Both create sensory markers. Writing down your goals in a location (e.g., a piece of paper) that is readily accessible creates an external storage source. As one writer said, "It doesn't take a neuroscientist to know you will remember something much better if you're staring at a visual cue

Tips and Tricks

(aka reminder) every single day." As you repeatedly read it, it becomes encoded in your brain through a biological process by which the things we perceive travel to our brain, where they're analyzed and either stored or discarded. The more you look at a goal and the tactics to achieve it, the more your brain will see it as information that needs to be kept. If you write it down, it is likely to be stored. If you repeatedly read it, it gets encoded. And that means it has a much greater chance of being accomplished. Once encoded, your brain and subconscious will take over, pushing you to achieve success.

It's easier than you think since you've been trained to do it. Think about how you work with clients or prepare legal documents. You listen, take notes, make checklists, check cites, revise contracts, and improve arguments—all of which you put in writing. So why not apply that simple skill set for your own good?

Watch, listen, and shut up. Remember when I mentioned the blinding glimpse of the obvious? The tip to avoiding a self-imposed slap to the side of your head for missing what's right in front of you is to learn to watch and listen before you say anything. Much of what we miss is because we make assumptions too early and jump into a conversation too soon, often interrupting the speaker. That's a tough habit to remedy and one I struggle with every day. But when I can control my desire to speak or interrupt, I learn more about clients and their problems. Obvious? Perhaps. But how good are you at watching and listening?

Here's a simple test on your powers of observation. Each of the famous logos below contains an intentional, subliminal message. Can you spot them?

If you haven't seen them, here are some hints:

- Do you see the skyline in the logo for the Bronx Zoo?
- Do you see the mother and child lovingly looking at one another in the Home for African Children Initiative logo?
- Do you see the arrow in the FedEx logo that lets you know FedEx moves you forward?
- Do you see how the arrow in the Amazon logo assures you that Amazon has you covered from A to Z?

Need more help? Here they are:

Use all your senses. Consider how misleading emails can often be. Most are written in haste and fail to give the complete picture. Don't let what you read mislead you because you make unintended assumptions. Instead, call the client so you hear, not just read, what they need. Or if you can't call them, ask for clarification in an email before you give advice. Or best of all, see the client face to face to observe how they communicate their concerns. Today, that probably means an annoying Zoom or Meets call. But it will be easier as soon as we return to normalcy. You can tell a lot about a person by hearing their voice or seeing how they react. That's one advantage of social media, where many clients and prospects post pictures and videos. Watch them and learn. Use all your senses to understand a client or prospect. Don't just read—listen, ask, and watch.

Never burn a bridge. If you decide that someone not responding should no longer be a target or should be removed from a goal or tactic, that's fine. But don't totally give up on anyone, and continue to include that person on your network lists and other general firm outreach programs. Keep in contact at some level. And never let your emotions cause you to say something to someone that can't be retracted and that will burn any bridge back into a relationship. Bite your tongue.

Don't do this alone. Most firms have resources to help you. Where available, they are resources you should turn to. There are also free online resources that are getting better as artificial intelligence applications are developed. Use all of them.

But most importantly, find a mentor you respect and who has the time and willingness to help as early in your career as possible. Or more than one mentor. You'll find it isn't hard to find such people. You have to ask. And while they're most likely to be more senior lawyers in your firm, they can also be successful businessmen or women you work with or know. Businessmen and women probably know more about building a business than most of the lawyers in your firm.

Try to have fun with what you hate. Most people loathe networking. I know I do. I feel out of place among people I don't know. Or I fear intruding on someone's "space" and alienating them. Or some people are just plain uncomfortable talking about themselves or asking for business. How do you get over those hurdles? Here are some ideas:

First, make a game of it. Decide before you go to an event that you will score yourself and consider it a "winning" night if you've talked to five people and gotten their business cards. It's even better to get a list of attendees beforehand and identify those you'd most like to meet.

Second, whenever you get a card, give a card. Be sure you have enough with you. I know—a blinding glimpse of the obvious. But how many times have you gone places without your business cards?

Third, when you have five cards, find a quiet place and jot down what you learned about the person on the back of the card or type it into a note on your phone. Later, you'll enter all of that in the notes section of his or her Outlook Contact. Here's where you can enter it in Outlook. Other products have similar fields in which data can be stored.

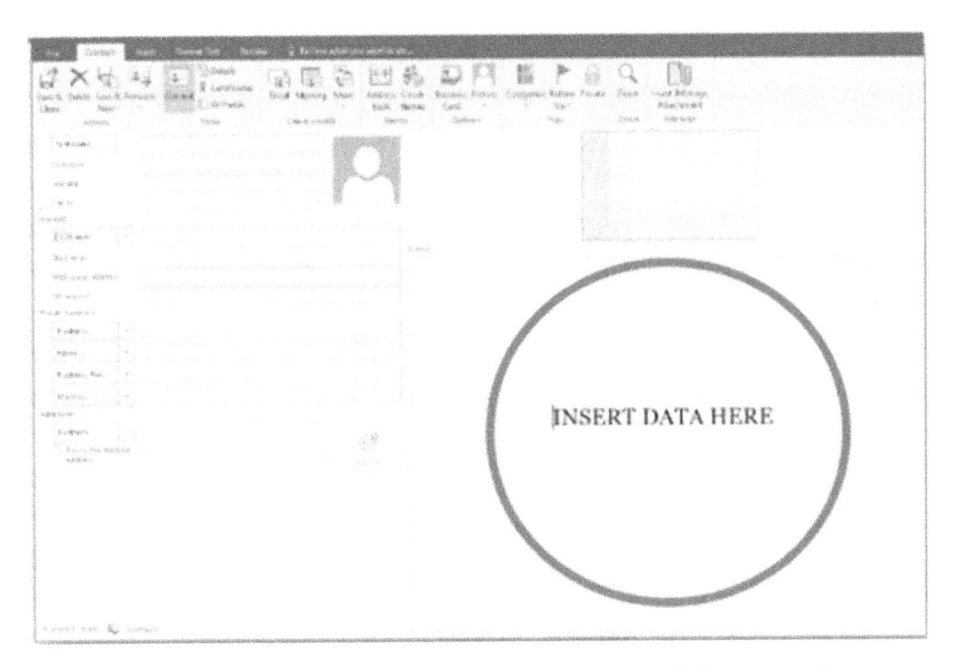

Finally, if you're up to it, go for a second round of the same. Repeat as often as you can tolerate. The point is to take it in increments. It's no different from an elite long-distance runner. They don't think of a marathon as a 26.4-mile race. They think of the first 100 yards from the start, then the first quarter mile, and then each mile one at a time.

Like any game, preparation is the key to winning. So if you can get a list of attendees, see what you can learn about them from a search on Google. You might find something in common. Or something they care about. That brings us to the next tip.

Get to know the person, then the checkbook. Before you ask someone to open their checkbook and give you work, you first need to establish a relationship with them. Ask yourself: Why do people like you? Chances are because they think you like them. That's the first goal of developing a relationship that might become business. The person needs to believe you care about them and their problems, and that you have empathy.

Think of the close friends you have. You likely feel close to them because you believe they care about you. While a traditional friendship with clients is not typical, the same principles behind your close relationships apply. If you want to be hired by a client, get to know them and let them know you care.

When in doubt, turn to Google. As I noted earlier, if you are at an event or meet someone professionally but wonder what they do, find a quiet place, turn to your cell phone, and search them on Google, Facebook, and LinkedIn. That simple step can reveal volumes about someone. But how often have you tried it on the spot to learn a little about the person in real-time? When you do, you can look for an opportunity to interject what you've learned. But be careful. Do not make it too personal and never ask about religion or politics, regardless of what they post on LinkedIn or Facebook. If you find nothing, that tells you the person guards their privacy. Be careful when talking to them and eliciting personal information.

For example, if you looked at my LinkedIn profile, you'd read:

> I've practiced law for over 47 years and am listed among the leading global specialists in advertising law in *Chambers*, the *Legal 500*, *The Best Lawyers in America*, and *Super Lawyers*. I am a member of the *Legal 500* Advertising Law Hall of Fame.
>
> In 2004, I and most of my colleagues from Hall Dickler, an entertainment boutique I managed, joined Reed Smith and founded the firm's Entertainment and Media Law practice group, which today is among the world's leading entertainment and media law practices. In 2024, I founded a solo practice and put Big Law behind me.
>
> I served as General Counsel to the Association of National Advertisers (ANA) for over twenty years and remain counsel to the ANA's Board of Directors. I am a Management Trustee on the Screen Actors Guild Pension Plan. For over a decade, I was the advertising industry's Chief Negotiator for the collective bargaining agreements with SAG-AFTRA, the largest union agreements in the entertainment industry. I am the founder and emeritus member of the Global Advertising Lawyers Alliance (GALA), an international network composed of independent law

firms that have expertise in advertising and marketing law with members from over 80 countries.

I am also a writer and novelist. I am the author of *Please Be Advised: The Legal Reference Guide for the Advertising Executive* (7th edition), considered (as Bob Liodice, CEO of the Association of National Advertisers said), the legal bible for the advertising industry; *101 Things I Want to Say . . . the Collection* (2014), a book on fatherly advice; *Presidential Intentions* (2014), *Presidential Declarations* (2015), and *Presidential Conclusions* (2017), an award-winning political thriller trilogy about the first female President of the United States; *Asshole Attorney: Musings, Memories and Missteps in a 40 Year Career* (2018), winner of the 2019 Independent Press Award for Best Humor and Wit; *Dark Data: Control, Alt, Delete* (2020), a thriller about terrorism's use of social media and winner of the 2020 Independent Press Award for Best Political Thriller; *Dragon on the Far Side of the Moon* (2021), a thriller pitting the United States and China against one another in colonizing the moon; *Blood on the Bayou* (2022), an award-winning novel set in New Orleans that pits a serial killer against an FBI profiler; *The Shakespeare Killer* (2023), a sequel to *Blood on the Bayou* that follows the FBI profiler on a global search for a serial killer murdering criminal defense attorneys and winner of the 2023 Independent Press Award for Distinguished Favorite in Crime Fiction; and *From Dawn to Dusk: How to Build a Multimillion-Dollar Law Practice and Then Give It Away* (2024). My next novel, *Deadly Bytes*, will be released in late 2024. All of my novels and many blogs can be found at www.douglasjwood.com.

I received a BA from the University of Rhode Island, a JD from the Franklin Pierce Law Center, an LLM in Trade Regulation from the New York University School of Law, and an Honorary Doctor of Laws from the University of New Hampshire. I have been an adjunct professor of advertising law at the UNH Franklin Pierce School of Law and the University College Cork in Ireland. I was on the Board of Trustees of the Franklin Pierce Law Center for over 20 years and served as its Chair for 15 years, leading it through its merger

> with the University of New Hampshire. I remain on the Dean's Council.
>
> I live in North Carolina with Carol Ann, my wife of fifty years, and I have three wonderful children, a terrific son-in-law and daughter-in-law, and five fantastic grandchildren. In my spare time, I work on improving my golf game, a never-ending battle.

My bio includes a lot of personal information that you can be pretty sure I'd love to talk about. And the more you get me to talk about myself, the more I will think you care about me. And the more I think you care about me, the more inclined I'll be to do business with you.

So what is the lesson?

Never start off telling someone about yourself. Instead, ask them about what they do and learn as much as you can. Wait for them to ask you about yourself before you volunteer that information. And when they do ask you, keep it brief and get back to finding out more about them. Be sure to enter everything you've learned about that person into the notes section of his or her Outlook contact.

But again, don't get too personal and creep the person out. For example, if you look at my Facebook page, you'll see that I recently had a grandson enter the world. You'll also see that I post very little about my personal life on Facebook. So if you walked up to me at a social gathering and suddenly congratulated me on my grandson, I might look upon you as a stalker or troll. Instead, try to move the conversation to families and if I talk about my family, you can then ask if I have any grandchildren. Ask name, age, where they live, etc. That shows you have an interest in me. And the more I think you're interested in me, the more I'll be interested in you. The more I'm interested in you, the more likely I'll turn to you when I need a lawyer.

Step right up and volunteer. Every practice area has a trade association representing its industry's interests. Get involved with them at some level. Offer to provide a seminar. Join a committee. Attend meetings open to you. Identify the opportunities to be in the room with decision-makers. Try to get your name associated with solutions, e.g., policy memos, business templates, etc., when possible. There is no easier way to network. These are all tactics you can adopt in your business plan. A word of caution. Don't dive into volunteering in associations of lawyers. That's like sharks swimming in a team and looking for prey. Stick to associations where you'll find clients. Where you'll find the people who write the checks.

It's a clusterf*^k out there. Breaking through the clutter that inundates our lives is a tremendous challenge. We all receive hundreds of emails daily, spend hours responding, become glued to our phones and screens all day, and now receive countless requests for meetings on Zoom, Meets, Teams, WebEx, and more. Your clients and prospects are no different. So, how can you break through that clutter? It is certainly not by adding to the same stream that diverts their attention. Emailing is no way to break the clutter.

Similarly, virtual group meetings need to be used sparingly as marketing tools. Invitations to webinars are fine, but unless you're the speaker, they offer no one-on-one contact. None of these technologies is personal enough to help bond you to a client or prospect. The trick is to develop ideas that distinguish you from the noise and get you noticed.

For example, how about going "old school"?

Remember when you used to say thank you in a personal handwritten note that eventually arrived in your recipient's physical mailbox? Almost no one does that anymore except perhaps to thank someone for a wedding present—and even that's fallen prey to emails.

I use personal note cards to write to a client or a prospect to say I'm thinking about them, thank them for something, or congratulate them on a professional or personal achievement. It gets acknowledged every time, a lot more than an email.

Tips and Tricks

Here's another. Rather than sending out traditional December holiday cards, I send out a printed card at Thanksgiving in which I thank those to whom I send it for a great year and let them know I've made a charitable contribution to a cause I care about to give thanks for all our blessings.

Don't you think you'd like to receive an "old school" thank you or a holiday greeting that's not an email flooding your inbox? I guarantee you that clients and prospects do. It breaks through the clutter. Use my ideas or think of others and share them with your colleagues.

Digital Decluttering. Also, think about ways to cut through the clutter on digital platforms. Use tools like LinkedIn more creatively. When you read something posted by someone you're trying to build a relationship with, don't just click "Like." Click "Share" and write something nice about the person as you introduce what they posted to your network. Make sure they see it. Better yet, post a robust and possibly provocative comment. Start a dialog. You can also target others who have left comments by adding your comments to their comments. If someone responds to your post or comment, respond to them. The point is to create a conversation, not just a thumbs up.

Similarly, if you receive a notification on LinkedIn that someone has been promoted, had a birthday, been associated with you for some time, etc., don't just send back the canned responses of "Congratulations" or "Happy Birthday" that LinkedIn suggests. Type in a comment that reflects more, e.g., comment on their career if they've been promoted, mention a nice memory if they're having a birthday, or the wisdom they've shared with you over the years you've known one another. The point is NOT to follow the herd, but to break away and be seen.

Although I'm not fond of using email for congratulations or holiday greetings, my former colleague, Mark Goldstein, sends out an email each year that does more than convey best wishes. He includes a list of fun facts he remembers from that year and attaches photos of his wife and kids with humorous captions. He makes it very personal. You're compelled to read it. That helps it break through the pablum others typically send.

All this interaction on LinkedIn will get back to many of the contributors and help build your network.

Another social media tool is Passle. It's a straightforward platform where you highlight a quote by someone else and comment on it. This helps establish your interests and expertise in the marketplace. In addition,

Tips and Tricks

consider focusing on quotes from people you want to know or reach out to. By quoting them, they'll probably notice your interest, or you can let them know directly and link them to your Passle post.

Always open the chat function on Zoom calls and watch what people post. Chances are someone will ask a question or make a comment to which you can respond. Better yet, you can include a link to materials you've published or resources you recommend. Remember that the chat room is as much a part of networking on Zoom as the call itself.

Last, with today's preoccupation with social media and videos (assuming you have good production skills), consider posting a video and sending a link to your contacts. Try to keep it entertaining and funny. That will get a better response than a tearjerker. Whatever you produce, do not make it political or religious. While you may have strong feelings concerning either, it's too risky. Keep those opinions in your private circle.

Avoid cookie c[l]utter presentations. Speaking of clutter, remember that propaganda from law firms bombards clients and prospects. If your pitches look like all the other firm pitches, you will probably find your proposals thrown in the wastebasket along with the rest. If you can, turn to professionals. Rely on them to help. If you or your firm don't have such resources, use your common sense and draft your pitches to be unique. Use good visuals, including charts and graphs. Remember that what someone sees can often be more powerful than what they read.

The first paragraph they read, however, is the most important. As noted, I am also a novelist. Every writer knows that the first chapter in a book has to grab the reader and peak his or her curiosity. If you fail to do that, they'll put your book down and never read it. It's the same for business proposals. Your opening paragraph has to distinguish you from all the others they're reading.

Alone is good; in pairs is better. Public speaking is a wonderful and time-proven method to build your reputation and reach prospects. Whenever you're given an opportunity to speak, do so, even if it's on a panel that includes some of your competitors. When you're given the honor of a solo gig, look at it not just to get a singular exposure of your expertise but also as an opportunity to directly connect with a client or prospective client. How? Invite the client or prospect to speak with you on the stage. Tell them you'll do all the work and make sure you give them time to shine. Not only will that solidify a relationship with the person you're partnering with, but it will also reinforce your reputation, since that person will probably compliment you on your abilities during the presentation. That's the endorsement you want. More on building and maintaining your reputation is in Appendix F.

Don't let disappointment be discouraging. You're not going to win them all. You've come far enough in your career as a lawyer to know that. You have learned to deal with the disappointment. Now, here's the rub—when you decide to build your book of business, you will face a lot of disappointment and not just in lost pitches. Sometimes, colleagues will let you down. Other times, you'll be shocked by disloyalty from a client or disappointed with yourself for not seeing a critical issue that later comes to bite you and the client. You'll need a thick skin to succeed. Persevere, and you will win.

Always ask why you lost. You will have your fair share of lost pitches. It goes with the territory, and when it happens, you'll come up with all sorts of excuses. That's a normal reaction. But rather than crying over spilled milk, call the client or prospect and ask for a debriefing on why you lost the opportunity. It may be as simple as price or as disturbing as a question about your or your colleague's capabilities or qualifications to do a job. Regardless of the reasons, three important things come out of such debriefings. First, you learn the client's or prospect's sensitive points. If they invite you to pitch for something in the future, you know you need to deal with those points. Second, you'll learn where your weaknesses lie and can take measures to correct them. If you can fix them, add them to your annual SWOT analysis. You may realize that those weaknesses can't be rectified and future business in that subject area is not worth pursuing. Finally, it will impress the client or prospect that you care enough about them and are ready to have an honest conversation with them. They won't forget that in future opportunities.

Regardless, you learn from your defeats. Ask any coach of a successful sports player, and he or she will tell you they learn a lot more from their defeats than they do from their victories. They also prepare by looking at game footage before entering the field of play. The business of law is no different. Do the same when you research a client before making a presentation. That's why successful litigators often ask jury members why they sided with the opposing party in cases that have been lost.

Always ask why you won. Don't limit your questioning to losses. Ask clients who award you a matter why they did so. What was it that put you and not your competitors across the finish line? More importantly, ask what you could have done better and what they liked about the other presenting firms.

Coca-Cola is not Pepsi-Cola. When I managed a firm in the late nineties, we renovated and included a concession area where employees and colleagues could buy light food and beverages from vending machines. As I inspected the completed construction, I noticed that the soda machine was emblazoned with a Pepsi-Cola logo and filled with Pepsi-Cola products. I was told it was a good deal. Turning to the contractor, I told him to get rid of that machine and replace it with one from Coca-Cola, a firm client. I knew that if folks from Coca-Cola ever saw that we'd installed a Pepsi-Cola vending machine, particularly because it was cheaper or a better deal, they would not have looked upon that with favor. While that may seem obvious to remember, it extends to more subtle mistakes you must avoid. For example, if you're inviting clients to an event you're sponsoring where a product will be served, make sure it is a product made by clients and not their competitors. Likewise, go out of your way when you're out with them to order their products. Better yet, order something new that the client is making to show you're staying on top of their developments.

When Scotland-based Edrington, owner of The Macallan Scotch and other premium spirits, invited us to pitch for their US business, I arranged a lunch at Sidecar, a club above PJ Clarke's, a local New York City restaurant. I liked it because it had a speakeasy atmosphere, which I thought the folks from Edrington would enjoy. The Global General Counsel and Chief

Financial Officer were attending. I instructed the restaurant to place a bottle of Macallan 18-year-old in the center of the table before our arrival. A bottle of Macallan 18 costs nearly $400 at retail and a lot more in a restaurant. After we won the account, I asked the GC what things we did that put us over the top. One he mentioned was the bottle on the table. No other firm thought to acknowledge them in such a manner. So we got to enjoy some fine whiskey and went on to have a long and wonderful association.

Even simple things like that can make a difference. As they say, it's the little things that count.

Don't tell me what you had for lunch. Social media mistakes make headlines every day. People think that the world cares about what they had for lunch, where they went for fun, who they hang out with, and just about anything else they can think of posting that frankly is of no interest to virtually everyone who sees it. The more dribble you post, which no one really cares about, the more clutter you create and the less likely a meaningful posting will be read. Please spare us all.

When you do post, be very careful if you post something about politics, family values, religion, and a host of other personal issues. Your feelings about such things are undoubtedly meaningful to you and perhaps to those who admire you. Today's world provides seemingly inexhaustible horrors to comment on. But as right as you may feel your comment may be, it might also alienate people and elicit criticism that can go viral. So be careful. Unless you're comfortable with what you post appearing on the front page of the *New York Times*, don't post it. Even if you do, think about what readers of the *New York Post* might think about it. Building a business is about making friends, not enemies.

I don't mean to say you should hide from the troubles that plague our society. Just be careful and try to understand both sides before you express whatever you believe, however calculated and intelligent you may think your views to be.

Find a niche. Think about niche practices within your industry sector. Most markets are fragmented into specialists with unique skill sets or challenges. It's also possible that a new shiny penny will attract a sector with legal challenges. Look for those opportunities, teach yourself the skill sets, and get ahead of it with blogs, articles, templates, etc. For example, years ago, while I was at Hall Dickler, AT&T and MCI started offering 900 telephone lines where a caller to the number received a flat charge on their bills shared between the provider (AT&T and MCI) and the owner of the number. It was the "pay" version of 800 numbers. Virtually overnight, it grew into one of the biggest marketing techniques in the country, with promoters offering prizes in sweepstakes, astrology readings, and more. Seeing it as a niche, we wrote a white paper on legal issues in the 900-number business. We quickly became the leading firm in the nation and made millions in fees before 900-number promotions were essentially regulated out of business. We had similar success at Reed Smith when we published a white paper entitled "Network Interference," a review of the legal impact of social media across many practice areas. We released it at the beginning of the social media explosion. It helped bring in millions. More recently, following an industry investigation of misfeasance and malfeasance in media buying, we focused on being the best in media buying contract negotiations by publishing a contract template, doing webinars, and using our PR group to get quoted in the press. While many other contracts are negotiated in the marketing industry, the most money is spent on media, so that seemed the logical place to go. Today, Reed Smith is the world's leading firm in those contracts.

Ask yourself—What niche might exist in your practice area? Where is the new shiny penny attracting clients and prospects you can turn into dollars for yourself?

If you delegate, you elevate. How many hours a day do you have to build a business while servicing your clients simultaneously? Also, you do need to eat and sleep at some point. Unless you're antisocial, eventually, you want to find time to relax with others. Even those who aren't antisocial need some "me time." There are just so many hours a day you can devote to practicing law. Somehow, you also need to find time to develop your practice. There are two ways to do that.

The first is to work billable hours until you drop. Let's say you can manage an awesome 2,500 billable hours in a year for a handful of clients you originated. You do virtually all their work, and they love it. Assume your billing rate is $500 an hour, and you collect 100 percent of every hour billed (a decidedly unrealistic assumption but fine for the example). If you can pull that off, your receipts will be a whopping $1,250,000 at 100 percent realization. Your utilization will be off the charts. That's certainly enough to get you a nice bonus, but it's not impressive from a business development perspective. Put simply, $1.25 million will not get you into the top compensation tiers of most law firms.

The second way is to delegate whenever you can. By delegating and getting others involved with your clients, you open time to find and develop more business. While others are adding to your book by the work you're delegating, you're also adding more value through the new business you're bringing in. So, the more you delegate to others, the more you elevate your practice. During my twenty years at Reed Smith, there were years when over two hundred other lawyers worked on my clients, all of whom were generating dollars that were credited to me.

It's not rocket science. It's a function of how many hours there are in a day.

It's not what you're doing that matters; it's what you're not doing that matters. Let's assume you've had some success with a client and have fee receipts of $300,000 from that client. Impressive, right? Wrong. If you have a client capable of paying that kind of legal fee, they likely have other legal issues you're not working on that can double or triple that revenue. Do some research on the client (or ask your firm to provide you with an analysis). See what other legal issues have been reported and what other law firms they use. If they like you enough to pay you $300,000, they will certainly listen to you if you ask for other opportunities. Now, think about my point on delegating. What better opportunity could you ask for than to build your book with a piece of business handled by your colleagues because you don't have the personal expertise to do it yourself? Over the years, as a partner, I produced millions of dollars for the firm year after year. Most of those dollars were earned by my colleagues who had expertise I lacked. Like I said, delegate, and you elevate.

Misers eventually lead lonely lives. Most firms evaluate an individual's financial contribution to the firm with both subjective and objective criteria. There is no set formula, and individual success is rewarded through a variety of considerations. The objective criteria include revenue from clients you originate, revenue from other clients for whom you work, billable hours, receipts realized off those billable hours, and more. Every firm seems to have its own formula. Recall my earlier examples of CRA, MOA, and MRA. The subjective contributions include leadership, community service, teamwork, and the full suite of attributes a firm considers important. Exceeding those criteria will best advance your career. It is a critical part of your business plan.

Clearly, the clients you originate are the most powerful lever you can use to improve your financial growth, but don't be a miser in giving credit to others. Share the rewards with those who help you gain new business and manage matters. If they know you're someone who acknowledges their efforts, they'll want to work more for you. You'll build a team of loyalists to whom you can refer work, knowing it will be done well. If you hoard the credit, your reputation as a miser will eventually catch up to you, and you'll have an increasingly more challenging time getting others to work on your matters.

It's not one-and-done. It often amazes me when I see someone do an excellent presentation and then do nothing more to promote it. There's a lot of fanfare leading up to it, and then crickets. Nothing could be more foolish. When you've completed a presentation, written an article, or been quoted in the press, push it out through as many channels as possible. Repurpose it. For example, if you've created a PowerPoint, post it everywhere you can. Better yet, turn it into an article and post it on LinkedIn. Send the article to clients. Promote the article on Passle. Get others to "like" and "share" your work. Why spend all your time producing a quality product like a PowerPoint presentation and only use it once? As motivational speaker and

Paralympic athlete, Josh Sundquist says, "1mt/1mt—one more thing/one more time." Keep at it again and again. If you do, you'll win more.

Let's roll the credits. I'm an entertainment and media attorney. Over the years of doing deals, the "credits" that open or end a production can be the center of intense negotiations. Everyone who contributed wants to be acknowledged. Even law firms sometimes appear in the credit roles at the end of motion pictures or television programs where they've provided services.

So, what does that have to do with building your business? Much like the note on misers above, if you hog the credits, it will eventually backfire on you. That applies not only to the objective standards but also to your general attitude of giving credit to others, both verbally and in writing, where it's deserved. For example, when you forward advice from a colleague to a client and take credit as if it is your product without acknowledging your colleague's contribution, it does not add to your reputation as a team builder. Tell the client it was advice from your colleague. Give them credit. Better yet, forward them the email itself so they can see what the colleague wrote. Doing so not only represents fairness to the colleague, but also introduces the client to the depth of your bench and the excellent resources surrounding you. And what does that do? It gives you someone to whom you can comfortably delegate work. It's a win-win.

Hey, I've been robbed! OK, you've done all the delegation you can and given ample credit where it is due. Excellent. Then you wake up one morning to find out that someone you entrusted with a client's work you originated is leaving the firm and taking the client with them. You might have any number of reactions, including anger, disappointment, fear, and a genuine desire for revenge.

Those reactions are a waste of your time. First, if you build a large book of business, you must give a lot of work to others. They will naturally develop their own relationships with clients and may become close enough to them to take them should they leave the firm. That is a risk you have to accept if you are to succeed. It eventually happens to every major producer. However, there are some things you can do.

Tips and Tricks

First, remember the fundamentals of business relationships. Even where you've delegated work, keep in touch with the key players you know at your clients. As one client said in 2004 when he stayed with me even when the principal lawyer working on his matters left the firm, "Doug, I came to the party because of you and have no reason to leave." When I probed him to learn why he stayed even though I had not done work for him in years, he reminded me I always stayed in touch on a personal level and reviewed his account annually. I stayed glued to him, so he stayed glued to me.

Second, I learned another lesson from that exchange with the client. I didn't realize I was doing an annual review. In truth, I was hounding him at year's end to pay his outstanding receivables. In one of those blinding glimpses of the obvious, I realized the client appreciated an annual review. It was another critical touch point that built the relationship and reinforced his perception that I was in charge. I later grew into the habit of giving all my significant clients a written annual review of our work and the resources we offer.

Last, when a client goes with someone else, never leave the client or your former colleague with a bad feeling. Always wish the client the best of luck and let them know you'll be there for them in the future if need be. Wish your former colleague the same. That can be hard in the short run but better in the long run. Be magnanimous.

It's a long game. We all know the expression, "Rome was not built in a day." But imagine how frustrated all the Romans were at how long it took! No doubt, many grew impatient and rode their chariots off into the sunset. The point is obvious. Be patient. It will take you years to grow a substantial book of business, and that assumes you remain diligent in planning and following up. But you will succeed if you put in the effort over the long term. If you're someone who needs instant gratification, find another profession.

Long shots. Speaking of long term, taking some long shots may seem exciting because they are. Think about how frenzied you get at the racetrack when your 50:1 bet leads the pack as the finish line approaches. But far more often, your horse fades away and doesn't even place—money lost.

It's the same if you go for long shots in developing your business plan. They might pay off, but rarely. So, leave long shots at the track where you can at least have a drink as you watch your money fade away.

Curl up with a good book. You probably read hundreds of pages of legal documents every week to do your job. You need to read updates and articles about your practice area. You might even find it relaxing to read a novel or two occasionally.

What's missing from those observations? Are you reading any books on business development? Most likely you are not. So, find time to read books by authors like Harvey Mackay, Romi Neustadt, Peter Drucker, or Barbara Stanny. When the COVID pandemic wound down, I read *Post Corona: From Crisis to Opportunity* by Scott Galloway. I've listed more in Appendix I. The point is to read books about business written by successful businessmen and women.

Or, if you're more into sitting back in a comfortable chair and watching TV, enroll in Masterclass and watch lectures by the likes of Bob Iger, Howard Schultz, and Daniel Pink. Watch the class by Sara Blakely, founder and CEO of Spanx. Her teachings are focused on entrepreneurship, but much of what she talks about are fundamentals of business planning you can use to build your own practice.

Tips and Tricks

While you're reading, consider some books that might seem less obvious. Two I love are Norman Vincent Peale's *The Power of Positive Thinking* and Niccolò Machiavelli's *The Prince*. Peale teaches us how to overcome problems by being positive, even in the worst circumstances, and Machiavelli teaches us how to win over our enemies by embracing them. A lot of what they write applies to building a business as well.

While much of what you read or watch may not seem to have immediate application to your practice, don't worry. Each book or video will give you a few nuggets to put into your planning. Be patient and remember that you're not likely to read or see how to hit home runs, but you will see how singles and occasional doubles win the game.

I've got good news. The adage, "I've got good news, and I've got bad news. Which do you want to hear first?" should be banned from your client vocabulary.

Think about it. Do you like to hear bad news? Do you think you can build a practice by telling clients and prospects what's wrong with something? Sure, some may accept the dire circumstances you can recite and even want to hear the downside to their plans or situation, but don't start with it. Litigators have a particular challenge in that regard. They have to think of the risks and challenges, but you have to approach it all with a positive attitude if you hope to earn the client's trust or a prospect's future business. I'm not saying to hide from the bad; just keep it as uncomplicated as possible.

Here's a scenario to illustrate my point. Assume you're at a cocktail party and get into a conversation with another guest who tells you they're considering starting a new Internet-based e-tailer to sell toothpaste. Pretty dull, huh?

I wonder if the first lawyers who heard about Harry's Shave Club selling razor blades on the Internet thought that was boring, too.

Do you think F. Lee Bailey, Johnnie Cochran, or Racehorse Haynes built their practices and reputations by first telling their prospective clients the bad news? Or did they start by explaining how they'd win a case?

It all reminds me of an old joke. It's sentencing day for a defendant convicted of murder. He stands with his lawyer at his side as the judge sentences him to be hanged at noon that day. He turns to his lawyer and nervously asks, "Now, what do we do?" His lawyer calmly replies, "Well, you die at noon, and I go to lunch." That will not give any hope—he's facing the hangman.

Always give clients hope. Never start with the challenges they'll be facing. Start with the solutions you can help them achieve. There will be plenty of time to get to the bad news.

Sorry, but I do have bad news. OK. I lied. I have some bad news.

Years ago, I was representing a large pharmaceutical company that had to fire over one thousand employees because the patent on their best-selling drug expired. They hired a high-priced consultant on how best to undertake the reduction in force. At the first meeting, the consultant said, "Remember one thing. You can never make bad news good. So don't try. Just fire them and give them an envelope with the terms of their severance. Don't explain anything."

I thought that was unbelievably cruel, and I doubt any consultant would be so callous today. However, it taught me a lesson. When you have to deliver bad news to a client (and you will have to more times than you like during your career), don't sugarcoat it and give the client more hope than is warranted. If his or her case is wrong, tell them. If they should settle, tell

Tips and Tricks

them. There is an adage on Wall Street that "Bulls make money, bears make money, pigs get slaughtered." It's wise to remember that if your client gets greedy, they'll likely be the loser and blame you. If he or she is greedy, they should not think that way because you gave them false hope.

I've had some fun with this concept. In my office, I have over two hundred pigs of all sizes on display. I love it when a client asks why I have so many pigs. I respond by telling them the Wall Street adage. They get the message. I've even given a pig to a greedy client. My personal note cards have a flying pig on them.

So be honest with clients, even with bad news. Over time, they will appreciate it far more than false, unfulfillable hopes.

If you don't blow your own horn, no one will hear you. Whenever you've done something for a client or your firm worth telling someone else about, tell someone about it. Don't be shy. Send an email to people about it. Let your colleagues know what you're doing. Likewise, if you receive any honor, author a blog, or are quoted in the press, that's probably fair game to post on LinkedIn. As with all social media postings, think first, post later.

Non-Billable Hours Earn You More than Billable Hours. If clients hate anything about lawyers, it's getting bills. We break down our time into 6-minute increments and often have entries at .1 or .2. It smacks of nickel-and-diming. Don't do it. Let those small entries go, or merge them into other entries for that day. While I never enjoy writing off time before billing it, you may want to consider letting some of the small entries go. They're not worth aggravating a client.

But there's more you can do with unbillable time. You can use it to build a relationship. Sometimes, a client needs advice on matters that are not necessarily legal. If you can become their confidant by offering your time without billing to discuss challenges, opportunities, etc., that will be time well spent, but make it a formal offer. Don't just do it and hope the client appreciates it. Be up front and don't be afraid to ask for something in return, e.g., recognition as counsel in PR releases the client sends out on deals, listing as their counsel on their website, etc. Over time, the "free" hours you've given the client will be returned in multiple billable matters.

Those who are proactive win. Those who are reactive wait. There is a big difference in marketing between being proactive and reactive. While the two work together often, true marketers know that a proactive strategy best assures winning. Taking the tip about blowing your horn, you need to reach out to clients and prospects on what you can do for them in their future challenges and let them know why you are different. That sounds simple, but ask yourself what proactive steps you're taking. If you answer that you send out firm bulletins, that's not enough. It's good but falls far short of what you need to do. You need to be seen as the expert, the go-to person for your clients. If you wait for them to knock on your door or for your firm to take care of it, you'll lead a lonely life. You need to knock on their doors with your personal brand, which brings me to the next tip.

Just who are you? Most lawyers are commodities. No one lawyer can stake claim to being the only person who can litigate a specific kind of case or negotiate a particular type of contract. Another lawyer somewhere else can probably do everything every one of us does just as well. So, how do you rise above the crowd and create your own brand? In marketing, it's called establishing a unique selling proposition (USP). The proposition is much like a trademark. It's what distinguishes you from others. You can do this through public speaking, scholarship, judicious use of LinkedIn and other social media platforms, trade or bar association leadership, community

Tips and Tricks

service, and more. A good business plan will include how you will become an individual "brand" among your competitors. For example, I wanted to be the most successful advertising lawyer in the business, but I had a lot of equally good competition. So, I wrote a book—*Please be Ad-Vised: A Legal Reference Guide for the Advertising Executive*. It was a lot of work, but I was the only one among my competitors who did this. That distinguished me and added immeasurably to my success.

One place to start with your USP is on your firm's website or other digital platforms where you post your biography. Look at what you have now. Chances are it starts like every other bio about the group you practice in and some areas you advise, just like every other lawyer on earth who does the same. No USP. Instead, start with something that sets you apart from others. By going to the site, the reader is already engaged and will read the balance of your biography for more detail if you start immediately with something that will grab them. In my case, I always start with my status as a member of the Legal 500 Hall of Fame for Advertising Law. While that honor may not mean much to some who understand how the rating organizations work, most people will read it as an accolade that sets me apart. How many lawyers can claim to be in any Hall of Fame?

Your office is another opportunity to create your brand. Make sure it is decorated with items that reflect who you are and your interests outside the office—pictures of your family, sports paraphernalia of your favorite teams. Make your office part of you. In my office, I have my collection of pigs, an autographed NY Jets helmet, an antique jukebox, original art, humidors, framed covers of my books, and more. My office reflects who I am. What I don't have are copies of my diplomas or court admission certificates. That's all business-related and things everyone will assume you have. Displaying them is tantamount to telling visitors you're more important than they are. I made one exception and hung my Honorary Degree of Doctor of Laws from the University of New Hampshire in recognition of my philanthropy for the school and legal community. That was an easy way to show the personal side of my life.

What is your USP?

Who do you think others think you are? What we perceive of ourselves often differs from what others think of us. Ultimately, what they believe is far more critical than what you think. But how do you find out what others think of you? You can always ask, but that's awkward. It also sounds as though you're fishing for compliments. An accurate assessment is the exact opposite. You want constructive criticism.

One way to get the perspective you want is to debrief with a client or prospect when they didn't award you an assignment. I talked about that earlier. Ask them why. They'll appreciate that you care enough to ask, and they'll likely be honest. By doing so, you can make a loss, a win. Another way is to ask someone you trust who reports to key executives. This requires a special relationship with someone and must be done carefully. For example, build a relationship with the CEO's executive assistant by learning a bit about them, thanking them for setting up appointments, and showing them some attention on holidays. In that case, you might ask the EA what the CEO says about you. You may be surprised. This is what I call working with the filters—those people between you and your client. Most executives are surrounded by people who support or report to them. Don't lose sight of their importance in building your relationship with the client. Make sure you thank them when appropriate. For example, in the United States, every day seems to be an official day for something, including National Secretaries Day. Why not send an email or note to a key client's secretary, acknowledging them? You'll likely be the only outsider who does.

Learn to say "no." There are some things you and your colleagues don't do or things you can't do at a price a client can afford. Sometimes, the best thing you can do to build a relationship with a client or prospect is to be honest with them in those situations where another lawyer or firm is better positioned to do the work. It drives me up a wall when a colleague suggests taking on something but discounting the fees so we get our feet in the door and can learn the subject matter. That might work sometimes, but more often than not, it's a recipe for excessive write-offs and disappointed clients. Don't get me wrong, I support discounts where appropriate for established clients and even to attract a new prospect. For me, discounting to get an assignment should be limited to clients who have proven profitable over the long term or a prospect where the long-term opportunity will provide an appropriate ROI.

But before you say "no," consider your options. The primary reason you should say "no" to a prospective client or "no" to taking on an additional matter from an established client, is because you cannot bill at a profitable rate. There are two things you can do. First, refer them to a lawyer at another firm who can do a good job within the client's budget. As a client once said to me when he felt my rates were too high for the matter, "I don't need a Rolls Royce when a Volkswagen will do." The client will appreciate it and remember your honesty and efforts to support their needs. Alternatively, some firms, like Reed Smith, have internal groups that bill at lower rates for routine and repetitive work. It's effectively a firm within a firm where one can refer matters that can't be handled profitably at the firm's established rates. These are groups of excellent lawyers at much lower rates but who, by their own choosing, decided not to be part of the competitive world of most full-time lawyers. The bottom line is that whenever you say "no," give the client an option to solve their problem. That's what you do for a living.

Don't apologize for your billing rate. Whatever your billing rate may be, it's likely based on a formula that supports the firm's overhead and adds profit to the bottom line. Private practice is a business, and profit-making is an appropriate goal. If your career brings you to the world of large firms, their billing rates are high for a reason. It's the cost of doing business and having the depth and experience to handle complex matters efficiently and effectively. Indeed, that ability sets them apart and justifies the costs. While I admit there are smaller firms or solo practitioners who can match the expertise and perhaps even the capacity, that is not always the case. So, when you quote your rate, don't do so with an apologetic tone. Your rate is justified. It's fair. If it isn't, you don't belong in the room. As your rate rises, take pride. It does so because of your success. That's not to say there are no situations where you can justify a discount, but you should never start a conversation that offers a discount before it's requested or makes the unfounded assumption that you're too expensive. There is another often overlooked advantage to a high billing rate. It elevates your image and opens opportunities to delegate work to others on your team without giving the client the impression they're getting second string. Assure them you'll review all the work and don't bill for that time.

There's more to CLE than CLE. There isn't a lawyer who does not hate CLE requirements. Many believe it's a waste of time to sit in a class or participate in a webinar that tells them what they already know. While some appreciate how CLE can keep them ahead of developments in the area where they concentrate, even they will say it won't fill all the required hours. I get it.

But another way to look at CLE is from a business development perspective. Think about what areas your firm works in outside your expertise. Take a few CLE courses. Then, when you're at a networking event and run into someone with a concern in one of those areas, you'll have a better chance of discussing a matter of interest to them in a relatively informed manner that may result in a referral of work to someone else in your firm.

The quid pro quo. Throughout your career, you'll deal with situations where you must refer out a matter or recommend a lawyer outside your firm. Conflicts, lack of expertise, geographic limitations, and more can dictate this. It's part of the business. As your career progresses, you'll likely develop a network of lawyers as your A-List for referrals. Developing such a list should be a priority in your planning. Why? Because it's expected that they will reciprocate, and the more work you send someone, the more likely they'll do the same for you with referrals. An extension of that principle is that if you've been referring matters to a particular lawyer and he or she is not reciprocating, ask why. Don't be shy. If they say they don't have the work to refer, consider finding another lawyer on your go-to referral list for matters of the type you've been sending. Don't waste referrals to lawyers who have nothing to offer you in return. Likewise, if a lawyer has been referring work to you, refer some to him or her when you can.

It's all about the numbers. Marketing expert Dr. Jeffrey Lant says that to enter a buyer's consciousness and make significant penetration in a given market, a brand needs to contact the prospective customer a minimum of seven times within eighteen months. By doing so, that brand will be at the top of the prospect's mind when he or she decides to buy something in that category. Why should selling legal services be any different? That translates into a simple tactic of making sure you have established specific ways you will reach out to your current clients and client prospects seven times during the year. That can be a personal note, a copy of a firm bulletin, congratulations on LinkedIn, a dinner, referrals, etc. It is not sending bills or updates on a current matter. These contacts or "touches" need to be personal and unrelated to the matters you're billing. They are added value to show the client or prospect that you care about them. Appendix B includes a matrix you can use to implement Lant's approach.

Create an eight-column bingo card. On the left vertical column, write the names of the key people you need to touch over the year. As you do so, fill in the boxes to the right of each contact. If you're diligent and fill in the entire card, BINGO. I guarantee you that will lead to business. Simple? Yes. Do you do it? I doubt it. I've included an example in Appendix G.

Conflicts can be costly. Lawyers run into conflicts every day. Your ethical obligation is to quickly determine if a potential matter will create a conflict with an existing client. It can be very embarrassing if you cannot clear conflicts as early as possible and most certainly before you accept an assignment or begin work. If there is a conflict, ask for waivers when they're permitted under the Professional Code of Conduct in your jurisdiction. Clients understand. Indeed, they appreciate it when you are up front with them about conflict situations, so be sure to bring up your need to clear conflicts early and seek waivers when needed. Mistakes can be very costly and, in the worst-case scenario, could cost you your license or bring about a censure or suspension.

Also, consider business conflicts. It may be ethical for you to take on a matter, but your other clients may view the work as antithetical to their business interests. For example, suppose you represent pharmaceutical companies that spend billions developing patents. In that case, they will not take kindly to the news that you also represent patent trolls who routinely infringe on those patents.

Within conflicts lay opportunities. When you are conflicted and can't represent a client, don't just give them the bad news and move on. If appropriate, tell the prospective client that while you're conflicted on a particular matter, you'd look forward to working with them in the future. Keep in touch with them. That's obvious, but go further and suggest a competitor or two who can do the work. The potential client will appreciate that and, if they go to someone you recommended, you create a chit you can expect to redeem from your competitor referring a client to you when he or she has a conflict. Make sure the competitor knows you referred someone, and as I noted earlier, if they don't refer someone back to you over time, then start recommending another competitor.

Be smart with your smartphone. Today, everyone has a smartphone. Get in the habit of putting appointments and alarms on the phone to be sure you don't miss something. Use searches before any meeting for updates on the client or other developments. Make sure you get your contacts in the phone directory. Download useful apps. DO NOT load your phone with games. They are too much of a distraction. Your phone is not a toy; it's a business tool. Use it like one.

Avoid asking questions at conferences. This is counterintuitive but important. We all attend conferences. A Q&A session follows most presentations. That's when an audience member can show how smart (or ignorant) they are by asking a question. More often than not, the question is answered by the person who made the presentation without a clue who the person was who asked it, even if they announce their name. Presenters don't register it, nor is there any follow-up, as the moderator usually moves on to the next question. I rarely ask a question after a presentation. Instead, I find the speaker at a networking session or in the hallway during the conference, exchange cards, and then ask my questions. By doing so, they know who I am. I might even get into a conversation with them. They also appreciate the fact that I've recognized them.

Tips and Tricks

We all love swag. Admit it. When you go to a trade conference, you love stuffing the conference bag with all the swag that suppliers give out. Even at smaller ones, you collect the pens and pads of paper. We're all hoarders. While you probably throw most of it away, you keep some, and each time you use or look at the swag you've kept, you're reminded of the person or company who gave it to you. It's a souvenir. In the legal profession, the practitioners who know most about swag are securities and M&A lawyers. When they close a new issue, merger, or other transaction, they love giving out bound books with all the documents or a tchotchke commemorating the event. Why don't other practices do the same? For example, buying engraved paperweights from an online supplier is cheap. Don't you think a client would like to receive a little gift like that? Think about it.

Believe in your team. Over the years, I've heard colleagues complain about some lawyers in the firm. I imagine that happens everywhere, and where someone lacks the expertise or understanding of a matter, such criticism is fair. But often, the criticism is more personal and exhibits more of a prejudice or bias against a person. They might not have a personality one likes. They might be too aggressive or too confident. Regardless, they need to accept that this is the team they're on. They can resist collaboration, but will not grow to their full potential without embracing it. That means they won't add to your success. Instead, make sure you tell naysayers you expect teamwork. You expect everyone on your team to give folks a shot. Make them part of your network. You may find out that while you won't have the naysayers over for Thanksgiving, you can, with proper mentoring, convert that to a true team player and trust them with your clients.

Work to live; don't live to work. While it's another cliché, life is too short. The reason you want to work your butt off is so you can enjoy your life. If all you do is live to work or if work has taken over your life, eventually you'll be a very miserable person (if you aren't already), and most likely a lonely one. While there are many ways to keep yourself balanced outside of work, e.g., sports, collecting stuff (like my pig collection), dancing, playing a musical instrument, writing, etc., the true question is whether you're having fun and enjoying your job.

While I am not so presumptuous as to suggest what you should do if you're not enjoying life, I will tell you that if you are not enjoying your job, find someone else to work for or something else to do.

I remember a junior associate who worked for me and seemed unable to keep up with the pace of private practice. I had an honest conversation with her and told her she needed to decide whether she wanted to give private practice a shot or find another place to work. She responded she wanted to stay. I told her that was great, and I'd do whatever I could to help her. She did fine for about six months, getting better by the day. Then she came to see me one day to let me know she'd taken an in-house job because she realized the pressures of private practice and multiple clients didn't make her happy. I was pleased that she'd put herself first. I wished her the best, and today she's very successful at one of the major credit card companies. She's happy. Are you?

Don't just believe me. Over the years, I've been privileged to count some of the industry's leading lawyers among my colleagues. I've also sat across the negotiation table with equally qualified lawyers who know how to build practices and organize teams. I've paraphrased some quips I picked up from them that I particularly like, a good number of which may seem obvious. Perhaps a blinding glimpse of the obvious (recall Harvey Mackay's advice). Or it might be a nugget that sparks a tactical idea.

- Program Google to give you daily updates whenever your clients are mentioned on the web.
- Attend your client's investor calls.
- Don't send clients copies of new lawsuits you've seen from reporting services. Many clients do not want to receive unofficial notices—as they may trigger expensive litigation holds before they're necessary.
- If you want to make lots of dollars, you need lots of clients.
- Believe that you are the best at what you do. Make that your mission.

Tips and Tricks

- Keep a sense of humor. You'll need it.
- Even if your firm decides not to invest in something you think offers opportunities, offer to put your own skin in the game and share costs. If they still say no, consider investing on your own.
- Make business development a mindset from the start of your career.
- People like to work with nice people. Be a nice person.
- The best way to network is to find an area you are passionate about and use that as the basis for deciding where you network and how you organize marketing events.
- Make sure your clients know you are there for them 24/7.
- Don't look for shortcuts. Hard work wins the day.
- Consider reinventing yourself. I particularly like this one. It requires real guts, but the rewards can be outstanding. I had a colleague with a large book of business that began fading as the company he represented split up. He moved his focus to AI and has built a major practice.
- NEVER, EVER look at your phone in a meeting. In fact, either don't bring it or turn the damn thing off. And by off, I mean NOT on vibrate. I mean OFF.
- In a meeting, assume everyone in the room is looking at you. Make sure you don't offend anyone or demean them by ignoring them. You never know who influences decision-makers.
- Don't be afraid to ask a client with whom you have a good relationship to help you build your business. Start by simply asking for their advice.
- Use collective pronouns like "us" or "we" when speaking to clients about their matters and issues.
- Play nicely in the sandbox, including with opposing counsel.
- If you're planning a trip, search your Outlook for contacts located where you're going. Look for opportunities to see them.
- Stay in touch with law school alums.
- Find out what a new business contact does for fun. Join them.

PART TWO: DUSK

Embracing Irrelevancy

Welcome to Part Two—Dusk. When your career nears an end and irrelevancy looms, you can fight it or embrace it. It's a tough conversation for senior lawyers—winding down a practice and moving toward retirement. For most lawyers, that is a challenging time. A lawyer's entire career centers on being an essential part of their clients' lives, often in a role far more than a mere advisor. Equally so, many lawyers have significant roles in their firms, guiding their own and the destinies of others. But the reality of age is what it is. Remember the adage that the only things you cannot avoid are death and taxes? Add irrelevancy, which is not necessarily a bad thing. It can be enlightening and exciting, particularly if you have planned it out.

You will see that this was a very personal journey for me as I departed Reed Smith after twenty years with the firm. I had to be honest and forthcoming to make it meaningful for readers. As such, I have related stories that some might feel are sensitive. Others may feel I've insulted them. That is not my intent. If I offend any of my former colleagues, it is without ill will or malice, and I apologize for any offense anyone may take. These are my opinions that others may find faulty. So be it. Undoubtedly, Reed Smith is one of the best law firms in the world. Its partners are leaders in the industry. Its management is concerned for the future of everyone in the firm. But nothing is perfect, and everything can be improved.

My hope in Part Two (where I use my journey towards irrelevancy) provides an example others find helpful as they embark into unfamiliar territory.

To paraphrase the words of Rod Serling, creator of the *Twilight Zone*: You are about to enter another dimension, not only of sight and sound but of mind, body, and soul. A journey into a wondrous land of irrelevancy.

The Reality of Irrevelancy

"Don't cry because it's over. Smile because it happened."—Dr. Seuss

As I look at today's legal and business communities, I appreciate the recent movement to address issues many groups in our society face, particularly efforts to fight discrimination, lack of opportunity, and other inequities. Many law firms, including Reed Smith, the last one I practiced with for twenty years, have programs to address the challenges faced by people of color and groups sharing commonalities, such as women, disabled people, veterans, the LGBTQIA+ community, and others. However, the issue almost universally ignored is the one in which we all, God willing, will eventually fall regardless of our membership in any other cohort: getting older. It affects every one of us, both personally and professionally. Yet society too often limits support for aging professionals (or just about anyone aging, for that matter) to how they can best vanish rather than exploit their years of experience, remain relevant, and continue to contribute to the success of a company—or a law firm—for which they work. Business today reminds me of the scene from the motion picture, *Judge Dredd*, where the aging judge takes the "long walk" and leaves the city for the Cursed Earth to disappear without causing problems for those younger citizens he leaves behind.

So, I have concluded that we need to add irrelevancy associated with getting older to the inevitability of death and taxes. In writing about my journey to professional irrelevancy, I hope others will recognize that cohort as one needing far more attention and support than it receives today as a group that can offer great insight and guidance in tough times.

This book offers ideas on how to make the journey rewarding and exciting. As Dr. Seuss most likely believed, becoming irrelevant is nothing to be afraid of, and, given its inevitability, you might as well do it enjoyably. That is best accomplished through recognizing the process and appreciating how everyone involved can make it easier and mutually beneficial. If you are lucky, you will do so with support from others who recognize their inevitable evolution to irrelevancy and appreciate you for whatever you've done to support them. If you're not that lucky, then you're on your own but can still win.

Putting modesty aside, it is safe to say I have had a very successful legal career, and my writing side hustle keeps my creative juices running. I am flattered by the reception from so many on "going solo" in 2024. I think I may be busier than I'd planned. We'll see.

For decades, I was certainly relevant in the legal community and assumed that would last forever or until I faded into the distance (health allowing). I'll tell you how wrong I was.

Rude Awakening

"The hard core of egotism is difficult to dislodge except rudely."
—Paramahansa Yogananda, Indian-American Hindu Monk, Yogi, and Guru

In 2018, I had a shock that made me think hard about my future and what legacy I wanted to leave to all the colleagues at Reed Smith (who made my success possible) and the many clients I admired. Reed Smith was facing an election cycle in 2018, and the position of Global Managing Partner was up for grabs if anyone had the guts to challenge the incumbent. While I toyed with the idea briefly because my ego demanded it (inflated egos are something that afflicts every lawyer) and was encouraged by a key partner in the firm to do so (more feeding of my inflated ego), I abandoned thoughts of such grandeur quickly, mainly since I thought that Sandy Thomas, the then-Global Managing Partner, was doing a great job, and I was actively involved in assisting in his previous election campaign. So, instead, I thought I would run for a seat on the Executive Committee. I had served on it before and thought another term would be interesting and exciting. If elected, I would sit for three years.

However, there was one problem. You had to be an equity partner to be on the Executive Committee.

In 2004, most of the lawyers from my prior firm, Hall Dickler, joined Reed Smith. I came in as an equity partner (the same status I enjoyed at Hall Dickler, along with two other partners from that firm). The other eighteen were associates, fixed share partners, and counsel. Given the revenue I brought in and the leadership positions I enjoyed, I assumed I would be an equity partner for as long as I liked. That was my belief until I read the partnership agreement fourteen years after I joined the firm!

Until you read the partnership agreement in 2018!? you are undoubtedly asking. Am I saying I did not read it when I became a partner in 2004? To be honest, I don't remember.

Even if I had read it, it was not negotiable and in short order, I would most likely forget anything I read, anyway. But since I was thinking about running again for the Executive Committee, I checked on the election process.

As I searched for the section on elections, I noticed a clause about what happens when you turn 70. The section, entitled, "Automatic Withdrawal of Equity Partner at age 70," provided that an equity partner, "shall automatically, and with no action on his or her part, be deemed to have withdrawn from the Partnership and shall cease to be an Equity Partner at the end of the calendar year in which such Equity Partner attains the age of 70 years."

I turned 70 in 2020, a year that brought us COVID and became an enormous challenge for all of us.

Since the Executive Committee term was three years, beginning in September 2018, I realized I could not run because I would lose my equity status before the end of the term. *Yikes!* I thought. *Am I that old? Am I politely being booted from the firm?*

As Chinese philosopher Lin Yutang wrote, "Sometimes it is more important to discover what one cannot do, than what one can do."

Once I got over the trauma of aging and realized I would soon be automatically de-equitized, it got me thinking about what I wanted to do with the rest of my professional career or, perhaps, my life. I suppose that's melodramatic, but that thinking caused me to recall what I had seen happen to other "old" lawyers I knew at firms where I managed or worked.

Short of health and other intervening events outside one's control, lawyers fall into three general categories. A few keep going strong, just like the Energizer Bunny, and are most likely destined to die at their desks. For some, that's fine. For me, however, they represent practitioners with nothing better to do. While harsh and not true in all cases, that is my perception. Some lawyers successfully do just that—the Energizer Bunnies, but that was not for me.

Another group is those who hold on too long and slowly wilt on the vine as their business fades. These are the tragic ones. The older they get, the further away they are from colleagues and clients. In short, they stayed past their "use by" date. Invariably, they become very lonely and bitter. That was also not for me.

Finally, some plan their future in an orderly fashion. They work out a deal with their firm and clients that allows them to continue working at a slower client-facing pace and undertake other responsibilities as they eventually reach a final exit from practicing law. I erroneously assumed such an option was common in law firms. I was wrong. Very few law firms pay any attention to planning for the retirement or ongoing roles of older lawyers beyond getting them to transfer clients to others. Surprisingly, I was looking at my options with little guidance from past practices.

I opted for what Reed Smith refers to as "Senior Counsel." In my case, and under the plan we agreed upon, that meant moving millions in revenue to other lucky partners. Most of them earned it. They had worked hard for my clients for many years, but until I moved those clients to their spreadsheets, they would never get full credit.

As I thought more about it and started on a plan, it hit me that I was intentionally making myself irrelevant in the firm and would eventually totally phase myself out of a job. I would eventually make myself invisible. How long that would take, I could only guess. Nonetheless, I accepted that reality. I knew I would become history, but I did so according to my plan and not the dictates of others and to have a good time doing it. Since I still had leverage in 2018, when a plan needed to be agreed upon, I was confident I could make it work.

How one becomes irrelevant is up to the individual, deciding whether he or she will deal with it proactively or wait until outside forces move them to obscurity. Harsh? Not really. It is simply a mature and healthy way to deal with moving on. If it makes you feel better to think of it in a gentler way than my tough love, please do so. Perhaps you prefer the approach of General Douglas MacArthur, who told a joint session of Congress on his retirement that "Old soldiers never die; they just fade away." There's also the variation on lawyers; "Old lawyers never die, they just lose their appeal." Pick your poison. It all works the same way.

I learned a lot along the way. In the following pages, I'll explain how I navigated change and offer thoughts on what challenges I faced, how I handled them, and what I and others could have done better. I hope they give readers guidance they can use on their journey.

Moving On

"Life is a series of natural and spontaneous changes. Don't resist them; that only creates sorrow. Let reality be reality. Let things flow naturally forward in whatever way they like."—Laozi, Chinese Philosopher

Succession (a friendly word for moving on) happens in one of four ways:

- Decision by management.
- Unforeseen intervening events beyond the control of management or the individual.
- Decision by an individual.
- By mandate under a contract.

If management precipitates the decision, it will invariably surprise the individual and create animosity. At that point, planning is nearly impossible. While the decision may be wholly justified, no one likes to be told it is time to leave by colleagues who are, more often than not, younger than they are. No matter how you spin it, it is the equivalent of being fired. Because terminating an equity partner in a law firm usually requires cause and a vote of the partnership, disgruntled management will instead try to force a lawyer out by reductions in salary or benefits. Nothing could be more demeaning, even when the reductions are justified. The worst of the four reasons succession occurs is management's decision (or indecision).

The saddest cause of change is, of course, unforeseen events: illness, death, disbarment, crushing losses, or colleague departures that result in lost business are some examples. No one can plan well for these events, but letting fate take its course is as poor a plan as one could have.

While a decision by an individual is okay, that decision often comes too late. Looking at the end of a career when you're doing well is not at the top of one's mind. None of us believes we are a commodity that expires. I certainly thought that way until I read my partnership agreement. Lawyers believe they can hold on forever if they keep their wits, or at least while they are healthy—the Energizer Bunnies. While some come to the inevitable departure decision gracefully, it is probably too late for a smooth program of change.

The last reason is embedded in the firm's contract with a partner, particularly among those with equity status. Many partnership agreements have provisions addressing departure and mandate a change in status at a set point in time. While firms need to be careful with such provisions under employment protection laws, they can deal with them through careful planning. If all the parties know about it, partners must comply. The smart ones plan for it. I firmly believe a contractual mandate is the best option. Had losing equity status not been embedded in my partnership agreement, I would have probably delayed the inevitable to a point where the timing would have been bad for the firm and me.

Therefore, with no choice on January 1, 2021, I ended my status as an equity partner and became Senior Counsel. Suddenly, I became a mere employee at will who could be fired for just about any reason (subject to age discrimination laws). That new reality, coupled with the 2020 pandemic and the sacrifices we all had to make, might seem overwhelming, but it was not because I had planned my status change for nearly three years. Instead, I embraced it with vigor.

In my role as Senior Counsel, I continued to service some clients. I also did more of what I love: mentoring younger attorneys, bringing in new work, assisting on marketing pitches, helping the firm in projects where it saw a role for me, and supporting the colleagues to whom I moved my business to build it even more. After over forty-five years of non-stop pressure from clients and colleagues, I was ready to welcome some breathing room while still taking on responsibilities that benefit the firm, my colleagues, my clients, and me.

Did I think being Senior Counsel would last forever? No. Could the firm fire me? Yes. Did I lose sleep over those realities? No. I cannot change any of that. So, what is the point of worrying about it?

Next, I go into the planning I undertook to control my destiny. I hope that how I proactively planned all of this will be helpful to others as they face their own journey to inevitable irrelevancy. Trust me, your day will come, but that does not have to be bad.

Planning

"If you don't know where you are going, you'll end up someplace else."—Yogi Berra

I began planning my transition when I realized I could not run for the Executive Committee. Rather than wait for someone from the firm's Senior Management Team (the "SMT") to knock on my door, I contacted the Global Managing Partner. We agreed I would work on a plan with Michael Pollack, a member of the SMT. Since Michael was assigned the job that led to Reed Smith's 2004 negotiations of its acquisition of my former firm, Hall Dickler, I was very comfortable working with him. We met twice, discussed myriad issues, and I gave him a written proposal.

The preamble to my plan set forth my commitment: "At a minimum, stay through 2020 when my equity status automatically ends. During this period, I will transition my book of business to other partners in the firm who are on my team. In September 2020, the firm and I will discuss any further relationship in 2021 or later on terms and conditions acceptable to both of us."

Some said that was perilous since by the time September 2020 came around, I would have moved most of the clients and have little leverage left for negotiating a deal for 2021 and beyond. That was a fair observation. However, I had faith in the firm's integrity. I took that risk. If someone lacks faith in their firm's integrity, they must approach the longer term differently and in greater detail.

The next step in my plan was an honest analysis of my strengths, weaknesses, opportunities, and threats ("SWOT") and what they meant to my future with the firm. Planning for my departure did not differ from the planning I'd done for years to build a practice.

A SWOT analysis is a business tool as old as dirt. Used in virtually every successful organization as a starting point for strategic planning, a synopsis

Planning

from a course at Harvard Business School describes it as a "Competitive strategy [that] begins with the iterative assessment of the external environment and the organization's internal capabilities. Strategic planners call this outside and inside look by the acronym 'SWOT': Strengths, Weaknesses, Opportunities, and Threats." While traditionally used by businesses, it is an equally valuable tool for individual planning. Being forthcoming about yourself in a SWOT analysis is often challenging, but it is a critical first step.

While one can often identify his or her strengths with ease, articulating weaknesses and threats is more complicated. In addition, whatever opportunities exist in your SWOT analysis, they can only be successfully pursued if you understand how to balance them against your strengths, weaknesses, and threats.

It has been my experience that most lawyers do not prepare a SWOT analysis for themselves or their business planning. That is true of law firms as well. That is a pity. I have started with a yearly SWOT analysis throughout my entire career. I predicate my annual business plans on it. Without question, I attribute my success to the SWOT and business planning discipline, so it only made sense that I would use it to plan my future with the firm and thereafter.

Unless you understand all four elements of a SWOT analysis, any business plan you create approaches tasks in a vacuum without consideration of your abilities to accomplish any of the goals you set for yourself. A writing I particularly like by an anonymous author reads:

> *I am my strength,*
> *I am my weakness,*
> *I am my opportunity,*
> *I am my threat,*
> *I am the reasons for my success and all my failures.*
> *No one else has anything to do with it.*

Next, I discuss the steps I used to establish strategic goals to address my departure, built on the principles of a SWOT analysis.

Mapping Success

"When it is obvious that goals can't be reached, don't adjust the goals, but adjust the action steps."—Confucius

Keep in mind that goals are strategic, not tactical. A goal is what you want to achieve; tactics are how you will achieve it. Understanding the difference is critical to success.

The difference between strategy and tactics is often confusing. Sun Tzu's *The Art of War*, widely recognized as the oldest military treatise in the world, may help readers understand the importance and difference between strategy and tactics. According to Sun Tzu, strategy is about winning before the battle begins, while tactics are about striking weaknesses. Put another way, strategy is an overarching set of goals; tactics are the specific tasks undertaken to achieve the goals. Changing strategies is like turning around an aircraft carrier—it can be done, but not quickly. You can easily adjust tactics as circumstances dictate; however, you must make direct changes to accomplish the goal.

After a reflective and honest SWOT analysis, my next step in proposing a plan for the firm was to establish my strategic goals. Here they are:

- The firm needed to incentivize me to move my clients to others.
- My team needed to be patient with the changes.
- I wanted to ensure continued growth in critical initiatives within our industry groups and markets.
- We needed to continue to recruit talent (globally).
- Everyone needed to contribute to the firm's growth.
- The objectives must be accomplished efficiently and economically by taking but controlling risks.
- The plan must be transparent and communicated to the SMT and my team members.

- Pretty straightforward. Let me briefly share my thinking behind them.
- *Incentivize me to move my clients to others.* This was the selfish part. I wanted to be comfortable. I needed my carrot at the end of the stick to motivate me to move forward without hesitation. I thought there was only one way to measure that—money. While I did not expect any of the bonuses I had traditionally received, I did not want my base income to drop until I had a deal for 2021.
- *Incentivize my team to stay and be patient with the changes.* I was blessed with colleagues who worked tirelessly on my clients. While they got credit for most of their work, every one of them knew the marketplace and the options they had. If they saw me moving without assurances of their employment security, all my efforts might be for naught. The firm had to step forward.
- *Ensure continued growth in critical initiatives within our industry groups and markets.* Investing in marketing and client outreach is challenging for any business, particularly a law firm. Budgets need to be managed. Doing so with hundreds of equity partners, all wanting funds to market, can be a nightmare, but for my team and me, a smooth plan depended on staying the course on critical initiatives and the investment they required.
- *Continue to recruit talent (globally).* I included this goal for two reasons. First, I could not be sure everyone on my team would stay for the long haul (and some did not). I believed we needed to recruit to fill any vacancies that might occur. Second, we needed to continue to grow. If all I did was pass on my work to a stagnant group of partners, the prospect of leveraged growth—i.e., using laterals to supplement fee income—would be illusory.
- *Contribute to the firm's growth.* While this may seem obvious, it is a good example of why it is essential to address the obvious. Of course, the firm and I needed to contribute to the firm's overall growth. But how? By including it as a specific goal, it meant executing correspondingly particular tactics to ensure it happened. It

would have been forgotten if it were not a goal.

- *Achieve the objectives efficiently and economically by taking but controlling risks.* A law firm is a business just like any other. Their product is legal advice, the worth of which is measured by billable hours converted to fees netted against operations costs. While revenue may also include contingency fees and other alternative fee income, most of what a firm earns is on the back of billable hours. Since a lot of time in the transition would be non-billable for both the attorneys being assigned the clients and me, it made sense that spending had to be kept under control and properly targeted.

- *Clearly articulate the plan to the SMT and team members.* It is risky to assume others understand someone else's plan. They may have suspicions or catch gossip, so they needed to hear it from me personally and from the Senior Management Team. Rumors are the most effective way to derail a plan.

- Some may think my goals were obvious, but time and time again, history proves that we often overlook the obvious to our detriment and only realize the error when it is too late to change. Planning—in writing—prevents that mistake.

- Next, I explain step three: adopting the tactics that ensured the success of my plan. In case readers have not caught on yet, planning is all about peeling the onion from SWOT to goals to tactics. Consider how you would apply the same or similar approach to your practice and firm as you absorb my thoughts. You may find it invigorating. or depressing. If the former, you're in good shape to start planning. If the latter, you must step up your game and make serious efforts to adopt a plan.

Taking Steps

*"Strategy without tactics is the slowest route to victory.
Tactics without strategy is the noise before defeat."
—Sun Tzu, Chinese General and Military Strategist*

Taking each of the strategic goals, I adopted specific tactics to achieve each one.

Tactics address the questions:

- What are you going to do?
- How are you going to do it?
- When are you going to do it?
- Who do you need to help you execute the tactic?
- Why will your tactic help you achieve the goal?

The "What, How, When, Who, and Why."

Each goal must have multiple tactics. The more specific the tactics, the easier to schedule and accomplish. The more details you provide on the what, how, when, who, and why, the more likely you will achieve the goal.

My actual plan had dozens of specific tactics the firm and I committed to undertake.

Every month, I met with my assistant, Nancy Schulein, and we exchanged emails updating the plan and adjusting the tactics. We kept adding tactics as I got closer to achieving a goal or was delayed in doing so. In 2020, the plan's final year, I submitted detailed quarterly updates on progress to the Senior Management Team, including financial spreadsheets and accomplishments. I updated management on how those who took over my clients were doing.

For associates on my team, I met with them once a month to go over their individual business plans, making sure they disciplined themselves. For partners, I met quarterly to go over their business plans. I had a structure that depended on the systematic review of written plans for all the individuals involved, whether they were lawyers to whom I was delegating responsibility or those who were accountable to me. Some elected not to take part in the written plan program. A couple dropped out midway. That was their choice. None of those who opted out received my clients in the transition. If someone did not commit to planning, I had no confidence they could manage and grow my clients.

Bottom line: If an attorney, moving his or her practice, follows my advice and prepares a SWOT analysis, strategic goals, and specific tactics, in writing, their journey will be far smoother than letting chance dictate their fate.

But, as the saying goes, it's complicated. Those complications, however, are not fatal. I like to think of complications in how watchmakers use the term to describe a fine timepiece: "It includes all the applications and technical solutions whose purpose is to implement additional functions beyond the traditional hours, minutes and seconds." Let's explore some of those "complications."

Attitude

"A positive attitude gives you power over your circumstances instead of your circumstances having power over you."—Joyce Meyer, Christian Minister

Early in my career, I represented Dr. Norman Vincent Peale. Reverend Peale is perhaps best known for his Christian ministry and his book, *The Power of Positive Thinking*. He and his writings inspired me to always look at life with a positive outlook, and thus his book was recommended reading for any associate who worked for me.

It would have been easy to dwell on the negatives in moving my practice. I was giving away my employment security. I would become peripheral to key management issues, excluded from decisions and meetings. I would be considered part of the "over-the-hill gang" and no longer relevant. You can add to the list. Put bluntly, I would eventually be forgotten. There is even a name for a fear of being forgotten—athazagoraphobia. If I cannot pronounce something, I will surely not be afraid of it.

Dwelling on negatives would have made the process more difficult and less likely to succeed. My change in status was a mandate of the partnership agreement. I needed to accept that to move forward on my terms. So, I was resolved to remain positive throughout the process and, mostly, kept that perspective. Indeed, there were times that I felt a tinge of negativity, e.g., when I did not get notices of meetings or I did not get return calls on what I considered open issues, but those feelings did not last long.

Some might say that such a Pollyanna philosophy is shortsighted and ignores the harsh realities we face every day. I do not see it that way, mainly because of my mother. What I learned from Dr. Peale, I also learned from her. Let me explain.

On New Year's Eve in 1970, my mother slipped on the ice while walking the dog. She crushed her spine in the fall and became a quadriplegic. Until that fraction of a second, she was a vibrant person. Now she was suddenly and permanently relegated to a wheelchair, no longer able to feed herself or take care of the fundamental needs of living a life. It would have been very understandable if she fell into a deep depression and gave up. She did not. Instead, she embraced the fate that befell her and became a leader and visionary for people with disabilities, counseling those in similar situations and helping others through hospice as they faced their last days.

Whenever I asked her how she could handle all her challenges, she would tell me to look at the situations of others who were far worse off. Doing so herself, she concluded she had nothing to complain about. She would tell me with a loving smile when I complained about something in my life, "Stop complaining. At least you're walking!"

She was a quadriplegic for nearly thirty years before she peacefully passed. I was by her bedside to share our last moments, something I will cherish forever. While I am sure she had difficult emotional and psychological moments in her private time, she was positive with everyone around her, including me, until her last breath. She was my anchor, and if she could live with what some might say was a Pollyanna philosophy, so could I. If you prefer to live in a world where you worry about everything around you and see people waiting in ambush wherever you go, good luck finding peace—or a reasonable road to retirement—with yourself and others. As this book continues, I'll dive deeper into that emotional side.

Emotional Challenges

"Life's tragedy is that we get old too soon and wise too late."
—Benjamin Franklin

Without a doubt, the most challenging part of transitioning my practice was fighting a feeling that I no longer mattered, that I was becoming invisible. In my case, while I do not think I fell into any serious depression, I was close. As much as I knew that what I do matters, fear of becoming irrelevant is an unavoidable and unsettling emotion.

As my plan unfolded, by definition, I lost control of my business. I was no longer in charge of the bulk of my former clients. I was no longer consulted on issues. I did not prepare many bills. I did not go to meetings. I was no longer leveraging relationships with the moved clients to build more business. In short, I was no longer doing what I'd done for over forty years! All those responsibilities were now in the hands of the new lead attorneys. For the plan to work, that was how it had to be. The new attorneys needed to be in control. In that process, however, I learned that letting go is easier said than done. You feel a real void. For over forty years, I built relationships with clients worldwide. Now, on a personal level, I was ending them.

As I moved clients and went forward with the plan, a strange sense of mortality set in. It was not unsettling, per se. Until I faced the logical end to my plan, mortality was something too distant to care about. While morbid, it is an issue we all eventually face. For some, facing mortality happens when they see their friends passing. For others, it is more severe through misfortune or illness. It was the realization that I was making other people richer and more important than I was in the relationships I created. I can only imagine how a psychologist would describe that! But I knew that at some point, I would become nothing more than a memory for those clients. It's inevitable. That's a lot for anyone with an ego like mine to swallow in one bite! It is like a parent taking their child to a neighbor to babysit and never seeing them again.

I dealt with it by talking to friends and colleagues in similar situations. We all know transition in one form or another is inevitable. I chose to do so through a plan rather than letting it happen on its own. While I thought what I did was best for others and myself, lawyers (like me) do not turn off a switch and become retirees so easily.

Do you have a plan to deal with the inevitable emotional challenges, or are you so confident in yourself that you do not need to worry about them? Perhaps you plan to just face them as they come. If that is your direction, I hope it works, but is it not silly to bet on the luck of the draw in an unpredictable future? As a character in the TV series *CSI: Hawaii* said, "Luck is a human construct designed to give meaning to random acts of chance, and in turn, comfort us in a universe that is inherently chaotic." I did not depend on luck.

Next up: Dealing with stress.

External Stress

"We must have a pie. Stress cannot exist in the presence of a pie."
—David Mamet, American Playwright

We all live with stress. In most situations, stress levels are similar from person to person, regardless of their chosen profession or activity. That assumes we measure stress by outside pressures. Internal stress varies substantially from individual to individual for complex physiological and psychological reasons far beyond the focus of this writing. Regardless, finding a balance between handling external and internal stress proved challenging.

First, let me deal with external stress.

In practicing law, clients and colleagues have expectations that build over the years as they become more experienced and deal with more complex issues. Eventually, if you are successful as a lawyer, you rise to a point where clients and colleagues come to you because they appreciate your years of experience and the wisdom that comes with it. While that is a wonderful feeling, it comes with its own stress—your clients and colleagues expect you to solve their problems quickly and efficiently. To make it more stressful, clients and sometimes colleagues come to you at the last minute with a major issue that could have been addressed more constructively had you been involved earlier. This increases time pressures and stress, often exponentially. As you climb the hierarchical ladder of a law firm, your billing rate also rises. That results in an interesting imbalance between efficiency and cost. Clients want lawyers with lower billing rates working on matters to save money. That can often result in less efficiency than a more experienced lawyer brings to the table. In the end, using less experienced lawyers may even cost the client more. Do not get me wrong. The quality of the work is consistent. It just takes more time and may cost more money. If I were to move my practice fully, I had to accept that whatever inefficiencies moving brought to the table, stepping out of the day-to-day practice was necessary.

In moving a practice, external stress comes from two directions. Foremost, the colleagues to whom you are going to move clients and the firm's management want the process to happen as quickly as possible. That is understandable. Drawing the process out serves little purpose except where a client expresses concerns (which, in my case, rarely occurred). The colleague wants to get the credit and build the relationship. You are under stress to get that done. On the other hand, it takes time and requires a commitment from everyone involved to be faithful to the process. I was lucky that all those to whom I moved the work understood and were patient. Likewise, the firm's management remained patient. That is why the plan's execution took nearly three years. The goal was to keep a forty-plus-year practice intact for the next generation. It did precisely that.

The second source of external stress comes from clients. After all the years I practiced, many of my clients have been with me for decades. With some, I developed a strong friendship (although I have rarely socialized with clients beyond occasional and obligatory lunches, dinners, and other events). They always knew I had their back and came to depend upon me for more than legal advice. When they found out I was moving my practice, they expressed their stress with change and pushed that stress onto me. That was predictable. They feared losing their consigliere and wondered if someone less experienced could bring the same wisdom to the relationship. In those situations, I aimed to ensure I instilled in clients an adequate confidence level in my chosen colleagues they could rely upon. That, too, takes time. It meant putting the colleague in a leadership position with the client that, over time, created the confidence level needed.

To relieve the client's stress, I assured them I was not retiring; I was taking a less active role, but fully intended to continue practicing law. I would continue to be available. That worked because it was the truth. I fully intended to continue practicing law for as long as I felt rewarded, just not at the same intensity. That meant identifying those few clients for whom I would still be available. Those clients fell into two categories: The first would not let go. That was very flattering and difficult at the same time because those clients are also among the most demanding of time and energy. But they are also important and need secure relationships with the firm. For those clients, moving them to others took longer. For most, two years of planning worked fine.

The second group of clients is those with whom I particularly enjoyed working. They were clients who came to me for high-impact issues—the "bet on the farm" stuff. Advising them keeps my brain synapses running and is important for me to maintain. There were a couple of clients who fell into that category. That does not mean, however, that they would not be moved. It simply meant that I remained a prime, but not sole, advisor for some discrete issues.

Apart from the external stress, however, was the internal stress. Dealing with my internal stress was far more difficult.

Internal Stress

"There cannot be a stressful crisis next week. My schedule is already full."—Henry Kissinger, former United States Secretary of State

Like most lawyers, I am driven to succeed with my clients and colleagues. That creates daily internal stress. When I added moving a practice, my stress levels increased because I was now dealing with something entirely foreign to me. I needed to move from building client relationships to letting them go. Doing this during a pandemic did not make it any easier. I was also doing so in an atmosphere where I knew I would soon become an employee at will, where success in executing my plan might also be equivalent to signing my exit pass. That yin and yang of the process created significant stress—stress to succeed and get it done just as I promised and stress associated with no assurance that my reward would be worth the sacrifice. Would we lose a client? Would the new lead attorney do a good job? Would the firm cut me off at the end of the program?

We each have different ways of relieving stress. As I did, you must find your own if you undertake a planned approach.

For some, it is exercise and sports. For others, it is reading a book, watching a movie, or sitting in front of a television set and enjoying your favorite show, newscast, or sports team. Better yet, for some, it is going to ballgames or parks to get outside for some fresh air. Your ways of relieving stress may be entirely different. Nevertheless, you must identify them and allow time to include them in your daily routine.

For me, I go out with friends, play golf (or try to), float in a swimming pool on hot days reading a book, take walks or bike rides, do crosswords, drive my golf cart around the community where I now live or, better yet, relax in the evening with a good Irish whiskey and a fine cigar. I sit quietly and contemplate the world around me without pressure to solve anything.

Internal Stress

While the whiskey and cigars are among my top stress busters, I am careful not to take them too far.

Look at how you deal with stress today. Is it working? Can you handle increased stress without a plan, outlets, or help? Think again.

Let's next talk about trust and how important it is to success.

Trust

"You must trust and believe in people or life becomes impossible."
—Anton Chekhov, Russian Playwright

There are more sayings about trust than we could ever quote. But without trust, Chekhov was right. Life would be impossible.

Those who were critical of the risks I took cautioned me not to trust the firm. More unsettling, some of them were significant partners in the firm. They believed that while some partners might make assurances or commitments to me, I had better get it in writing if I was smart. However, the idea that I was in negotiations with an adverse party and needed to memorialize everything in a contract was anathema to me. I prefer to believe in people until they prove I should not. While God knows I have run into some who screwed me (or tried to), they were few. When it happens, I write it off to experience and move on.

A psychologist once asked me why I was so accommodating to people. Why do I so readily trust them? I told her I have low expectations of others. I am unsure why I feel that way, but I am rarely surprised when someone lets me down. I dislike it and the person might disappoint me. But, as the AA motto reads, "God, grant me the serenity to accept the things I cannot change, the courage to change the things I can, and the wisdom to know the difference." It is a chore to change people. Accepting them for what they are and moving on when you realize they do not care about you is easier. Some may say that's naïve, but I've moved on from very few people in my life, and while I was glad when I did, I trust far more people than I distrust.

I trusted the firm. They did not let me down, at least in the beginning. Would I have liked more money? I suppose. Everyone wants more money. But measuring where I ended up and the firm's trust in me, we all found a good place, albeit with a few bumps along the way.

I am not sure if other law firms approach retirement or change of status of partners similarly. When I began the journey, I contacted several retirement consultants and my banker to see what other law firms were doing. To my surprise, they all reported that law firms had no real programs. Most did not address it at all, and those that did were anything but creative and compassionate. For most, it was just sitting back and leaving how lawyers phased out of their firms to fate. Often in my years practicing law, I wondered about some folks who left in their late fifties and sixties. Where did their firms fail? Or were they too shortsighted to see another, less traumatic way out?

I hope this book spurs conversation on this issue. It's long overdue.

You need to decide who you want to trust. Sometimes, that list may be short. Setting the parameters of your plan in writing is a smart move. Written formalities (other than your own written plan) may be unnecessary in different cases. Alternatively, you may want a hybrid through correspondence. If you think you can trust no one, then your plan probably needs to be more selfish and directed to leaving with whatever you can, assuming, of course, you did not wait too long to make that decision.

Next, I discuss the role of loyalty.

Loyalty

"Loyalty is a fine quality, but in excess it fills political graveyards."
—Neil Kinnock, British Politician

In my career, some criticize me for being too loyal to colleagues who later turn out to be untrustworthy, or for sticking with clients who have no appreciation for my loyalty to them or lack respect for my work. It is admittedly one of my faults. I have a deep feeling of faith—loyalty—in others, particularly colleagues. At least until they show their disloyalty to me. As you journey through the process, you need to be prepared for some rude awakenings as you see those you thought were loyal turn out to be selfish and fully prepared to speed up your exodus to irrelevancy.

Neil Kinnock, the colorful member of Great Britain's Labour Party quoted above, said this about the loyalty dilemma: "I warn you not to be ordinary, I warn you not to be young, I warn you not to fall ill, and I warn you not to grow old." Each of his warnings is a litmus test of loyalty and is often the moment we see people abandon others for their self-interests, most likely believing it is fair to do so under ordinary youth, illness, or aging circumstances. No doubt, Kinnock might add, "I warn you never to let anyone know you're retired."

As I transferred my practice, all my close colleagues remained loyal. After all, they had something to gain by being so. Once my plan was completed, I saw some lose that sense of loyalty as they marginalized my contributions or wholeheartedly pushed me out of client interaction.

Unlike in the earlier days of my career, my reaction surprised me. In the end, it did not bother me. It did not make me less loyal to them. I remembered that, unlike people who were disloyal to me when I had an active practice and was competing—internally and externally—for recognition and compensation, this new group of loyalists were the people I entrusted with my legacy (for whatever it was worth). To feel fulfilled, I needed them to succeed—even if it meant I would be one of those who, as Kinnock might say, filled a graveyard.

Mostly, my clients also remained loyal to me and the colleagues to whom I transitioned the accounts. A couple, however, despite decades of loyalty to them, turned out to be Judas. At first, that disappointed me. But then I reflected on a lawyer's role and remembered a story about William Paley, a legendary broadcaster who ran CBS for decades, turning it into the "Tiffany Network" with legendary programming. When Paley was chairman of the board, a fellow board member was Ralph Colin, CBS's general counsel for over forty years. One would think that reflected great loyalty. Perhaps it did in Colin's eyes, but not in Paley's. When Colin disagreed with Paley during a Board meeting, Paley immediately fired him. Stunned, he asked Paley why, after so many years as friends, he so unceremoniously dismissed him. Paley allegedly replied, "I have never regarded you as a friend—only an employee."

So be ready to swallow your pride and face some disappointments. Just don't waste your time ruminating over them. That brings me to dealing with disappointment.

Disappointment

"In the end, just three things matter: How well we have lived. How well we have loved. How well we have learned to let go."
—Jack Kornfield, Author and Teacher of Buddhism

Any successful person in business faces disappointments with themselves and with others. Clients can disappoint you when they fail to appreciate the work. Colleagues can disappoint you when they fail to do the job needed. You disappoint yourself when you miss something important or get blindsided by something you should have expected.

I would be lying if I denied that some people disappointed me. Some did so by marginalizing or rejecting what I suggested, others by outright ignoring me, or, worse, criticizing what I was doing behind my back. Did they think I would not find out? Suffice it to say, the walls talk a lot more than people think they do.

Some clients have also disappointed me. While they understood my desire to transfer them to younger attorneys, ready to build relationships, some fell prey to economics, finding firms that would cost less. While that was a very small number of clients, it hurt that they saw me and the firm as a commodity that should be rewarded to the lowest bid. To them, I wished them well. For most clients, the key to my success was being honest with them and telling them what would happen well in advance. That eliminated surprises. Most businesspeople understand change because their companies have established succession and promotion plans. They do not want surprises. They get it. Most law firms do not.

I had some disappointment with the firm, but it was more about process than substance. Because of the COVID pandemic and other intervening priorities, I was not at the top of management's to-do list. As a result, the firm delayed the resolution of my post–2020 relationship as senior counsel longer than I would have liked, but in the end, we got it done.

Disappointment

Some colleagues disappointed me, particularly those who chose not to embrace written business plans and meeting schedules. The prospect of being given active clients and the opportunity to build from a base in the millions of dollars excited more than enough of my colleagues eager for the chance. I moved my practice to that group. I left those who chose not to take part on their own. They have their way of looking at things, and that is okay with me. Who knows? Maybe my approach to planning is unnecessary to succeed. Maybe it is more a function of luck or just working hard, but I doubt it.

I had one serious disappointment with myself. I let the firm delay decisions too long and put myself at risk of not knowing what my future held. I did not get a 2021 deal until January of that year, weeks after automatically converting to non-equity status. I did not establish my 2022 deal until late December 2021. My 2023 deal took until February 2023 to get done, but more on that later.

But I was never blindsided. Why? Because I had a written plan where I took contingencies into account. I planned for the worst outcomes. That does not mean I might not have done better had things happened sooner, but on measure, the experience has been fine (admittedly in hindsight). However, I know the disappointments would have been more frequent if I had not had a written plan accepted by the firm during the transition years and a post-equity status personal plan.

The flip side of disappointment is anger. I will deal with that next.

Anger

"Nobody's angry all the time, unless you're a psycho."
—Brian Azzarello, American Comic Book Writer

The line between disappointment and anger is a very fine one, particularly if someone repeatedly disappoints you. Disappointment mostly led me to dismiss someone or just walk away. Anger breeds a need for revenge or retribution, which is why it can be so destructive.

Throughout all of this, I did my best not to get angry. That does not mean I did not get angry; it means just that I tried to control it as best I could. While Brian Azzarello's quote is humorous, it has a genuine ring of truth. Anger can become all-consuming.

As I journeyed through the process, anger took two forms—anger with someone else and anger with myself. I dealt with each differently.

When I was younger, I tried to overcome my anger with people by convincing them I was smarter than they thought I was and worthy of their admiration, or I would spend an inordinate amount of energy hell-bent on beating them. For me, it was a competition. In hindsight, I see today how naïve that was. Such a waste of valuable time!

As my career unfolded and I became more successful, if my anger with someone got to a point where I was having difficulty suppressing it and lost objectivity, my remedy was to remove that person from my life as much as possible. I have done this most of my career. It is harsh for sure, but as the saying goes, they are dead to me. I blocked them from my email and phone. I deleted them from my contacts. I unfriended them if they were a "friend" on Facebook or other social media platforms. I do not talk about them. I avoided talking to them. In one extreme example, I even instructed my travel agent (who handled firm travel) to ensure I never flew on the same plane or stayed in the same hotel as the person I wanted out of my life. I no longer wanted to waste time thinking about them.

Anger

In short, I distance myself from such people as much as possible because seeing them, digitally or otherwise, only feeds the anger and distracts me from what makes me happy. At my age, I would rather be happy than angry.

It is a brief list, and I will not recite the names of those I banished from my life. They do not care; I doubt they even realize they are blocked or unfriended. All I know is that "out of sight, out of mind" can be exhilarating. Try it.

Eliminating anger with myself, however, was a lot harder. I cannot delete, block, or unfriend myself. I get angry with myself for repeatedly doing unproductive, shortsighted, or just plain stupid things. Sometimes that happens when I promise more than I can realistically deliver, letting others screw up my day with unreasonable requests or frustration when dealing with people who are not listening to me (even if they may have their own reasons not to). It can manifest itself in my being angry with myself because I did not push someone harder, let someone get away with too much, or put up with someone's laziness for too long. During the transition process with Reed Smith, I forgave too many last-minute meeting cancellations or outright no-shows. I forgave not getting return phone calls or emails despite multiple requests.

I would sometimes hear myself ask, "Why do I put up with this shit?" Often, it was because I had no choice. Early in my career, when I was not financially independent, I was smart enough to know that moving to another firm would only expose me to other reasons to be angry with myself. It is an emotion you cannot easily control. In the past, I would just keep at it until I either solved the situation and rid myself of the anger or said, "screw it" and moved on. For me, it was succeeding, overcoming the odds, accepting defeat, and not getting angry at myself (and probably with others) yet again.

As I executed the plan, however, I found I was less and less angry with myself regardless of the disappointments I faced. In retrospect, I think it is because I finally resigned myself to the inevitability of irrelevancy and decided there was no reason to fight it. My financial independence was a significant factor as well. In one sense, it is ironic. We work our asses off to be independent, yet in the end, we cannot easily let go of the chains of work that prevent us from achieving that goal.

Was I ready to move in 2020? Probably not. Turning seventy was irrelevant to my ability to be productive under the standards set by the firm—revenue, billable hours, and productivity. I could have gotten angry with the firm for unceremoniously moving me out or angry with myself because I could have taken my business elsewhere and continued to work my ass off. Instead, the firm let me execute my plan, my choice. I cannot be angry with the firm for ending my equity partner status. After all, I agreed to it when I signed the partnership agreement. In hindsight, I am not angry that I have moved on to a less pressurized life.

Next, I will talk about the best anecdote for disappointment and anger—humor.

Humor

"Never take life seriously. Nobody gets out alive anyway."—Anonymous

I believe the ultimate elixir for depression, stress, and pressure is humor. If you can keep a sense of humor, dealing with challenges and defeats is far easier. A lot of this stems from my mother, about whom I wrote earlier. She always had a wonderful sense of humor. When she tragically became a quadriplegic, I remember thinking that there could be nothing humorous left in her life. Then, one day, while visiting her in the hospital, she told me to tweak her nose. I asked why. She told me to do what she said. So, I tweaked her nose. When I did, myriad machines monitoring her vital functions sent out alarms, and within seconds, a nurse arrived. My mom thought it was hilarious how freaked out the nurses were as they ran into the room. Since she was a registered nurse herself, I guess it was okay. It shocked me. Then she said, "Hey, smile. That was pretty funny." All the sadness I felt for her instantly dissipated into thin air. If she could get through her challenges with her sense of humor, anyone could.

Two more stories about my mom.

On another visit to her in the hospital ward filled with soldiers returning from the Vietnam War with horrendous injuries, I asked her how she could get through the pain and fears she must be enduring. She told me to look around the ward. She said, "Those soldiers are suffering a lot more than me." Then she smiled and said, "So, what do I have to complain about?"

When she finally reached rehab, they gave her an electric wheelchair. Learning how to use it was a challenge, given her limited use of her arms and hands. One afternoon, the nurses put her in a wheelchair to teach her how to operate it. When she hit the forward lever, she flew down the hallway and crashed into the wall. They all rushed to her, fearful she had hurt herself. When asked if she was okay, she smiled and responded, "What's the worst that could happen? I become a cripple?" While one would not use the word "cripple" in today's world (and thankfully so), you get the idea of how she approached life and instilled in me an equally positive and humorous way of overcoming challenges.

She lived to be eighty-eight and passed away peacefully in 2004. A quadriplegic for thirty-four years (maybe a Guinness world record), she never lost her sense of humor and resolve that she would overcome whatever challenges fate gave her. To put it mildly, she inspired anyone who ever had the honor of knowing her.

So whenever I felt challenged during the process, I thought of her and her ever-present smile. Find someone like that for yourself, someone who you admire and of whom the mere mention brings a smile to your face.

As you search for those people, you'll also meet some jerks. I will deal with that next.

Jerks

*"Before you diagnose yourself with depression or low self-esteem,
first make sure you are not, in fact, surrounded by jerks."*
—*Sigmund Freud, Austrian Neurologist*

In late 2003 and early 2004, Reed Smith courted me. Two other firms were in the mix: Arnold & Porter and Alston & Bird. All three are great firms. When I first worked with Nancy Wadler, the recruiter I hired for the search, I told her I did not want to deal with any firm "born" in New York or Los Angeles, noting that I thought they were all essentially assholes. I had seen enough of that in my years practicing in New York City and opening an office in Beverly Hills. I wanted nothing to do with that kind of homegrown regime.

At all three firms, I met many partners, but one thing that struck me was how caring and welcoming all the partners from Reed Smith were. How much money I could make them was not the first thing they wanted to talk about. They truly wanted to know about all twenty-two of the lawyers from Hall Dickler who were coming with me. I recall asking where Reed Smith's jerks were, assuming every firm had them. We certainly had some at Hall Dickler. I will never forget being told that Reed Smith did not have any. They did not tolerate them. In fact, at midnight hour before we announced the deal, I was told that one partner in my group was unwanted because he was a jerk to some staff members during his interviews. The firm was right, and I did not cry when we excluded him from the deal.

My realization of the ethos of Reed Smith and its roots in Pittsburgh came quickly after I joined. The firm had about 900 lawyers and I was told I could send a block email to all of them if I was looking for help. In the first week, I had an occasion to ask about a legal issue involving a major league baseball team I was battling over a client's marketing rights agreement with them. I asked, "Does anyone know . . ." adding the facts at issue.

Within minutes, I received at least five emails that began, "Doug, welcome to the firm. Just so you know, when we ask a question by email, we like to begin an email with, 'pardon the interruption.'" As a New Yorker, my first response was WTF is this person talking about? Then I realized it was their way of politely telling me that Reed Smith was founded on collegiality and expected it throughout the organization. It was a refreshing awakening for someone like me who had become somewhat jaded in the cutthroat atmosphere that pervades New York City law firms.

While Reed Smith, now with over 1700 lawyers, has lost some of its collegiality and collected a few jerks during its growth, I can honestly say I did not meet many during my change of status and movement of my clients. That was partly because I chose not to deal with anyone who was a jerk. Others might not be so lucky. I did hear stories of some who spoke unkindly about my compensation or the choices of new lead attorneys to whom I moved clients because they thought they deserved the role or had better ideas on succession. Some simply begrudged what I was being paid. They should have spoken to me directly and not been critical or jealous behind my back. I would have been happy to explain my choices. I would have told them to read my plan. It was all there, as plain as could be. I would tell them that those to whom I moved clients had to earn it by showing a commitment to the client over the plan term. They should ask what they could do to deserve the work and how to get to know the clients. In addition, just because someone has the most billable hours for a client over the past year does not make him or her a logical choice to inherit managing that client. The nature of the matter where they billed hours may be tangential to the day-to-day activities and management of the account.

That is the reason I was transparent with the plan. Everyone knew what I expected.

I admit, however, that I occasionally asked myself whether I was being a jerk regarding my plans. Such self-questioning is normal. Some of the choices as to whom to transfer a client were tough. I tried to be objective but admit I may have made some mistakes. In the end, however, it all balanced out, and the future was bright for all the attorneys to whom I moved the work. I can honestly say there is not one jerk among them—yet.

Next, I'll talk about the importance of diversions. It helps iron out the bumps in the road ahead.

Diversions

"I believe every human has a finite number of heartbeats. I don't intend to waste any of mine."—Neil Armstrong, *Astronaut*

You need to have diversions to occupy your time. If you transition properly, you will have time to fill. If you find the time to add diversions when you're no longer working your ass off, the process is a lot easier.

In my case, writing novels was and continues to be my prime diversion. It allows me to be creative and keeps my brain working in various directions. It is cathartic. I have written novels focused on politics, science fiction, humor, and crime. I wrote a memoir about the first forty years of my career, which won a prestigious award for best wit and humor. I am obsessed with developing book ideas. They often come to me in the middle of the night. My books may never be on the *New York Times* Bestseller List or find their way to the silver screen, but they are rewarding for me.

It is hard to write a novel. Try it sometime if you do not believe me, but it is fun to create characters and occasionally kill them off. I suspect the names of some of those reading this are among the names I used in my books for the good guys and the bad guys. I used to raffle off having someone's name in a book at Reed Smith's annual holiday party. We donated the proceeds from the raffle to charity. All three times, when I offered to name a character after someone, they chose to be a villain. When I explained to them that being a villain probably meant they would die in the book, they became more committed to coming to an unceremonious end.

On other occasions, I used the names of people I knew just to have fun. I named a lowly clerk after Reed Smith's Global Managing Partner. I blew up a few of my colleagues into smithereens in some of the more violent parts of the stories. The list goes on. The business of lawyers is to deal with reality. A fiction writer deals with fantasy. For me, it is a wonderful way to balance my life and relieve pressure.

Diversions

Now that the plan to move my clients is over, I write blogs associated with the subjects of my books. They are all posted on my personal website (www.douglasjwood.com) and on social media. While I do not have many followers (a few thousand), they are loyal and give me great feedback.

I'm also counseling and mentoring younger lawyers trying to build practices and older ones dealing with transition. It all allows my lawyer's ego to express itself. Whether I am imparting valuable information is for others to decide, but it is a way I pay it forward.

Last, I'm doing a limited amount of legal work that I chose to do.

You need to find your balance. It may be letting go completely, watching the sun rise and set. If that's what you want, great—If you want something more exciting, you have to start planning for it, and the sooner, the better.

Regardless, I am not sure I could have pulled off the transition so effectively if I did not have my writing and mentoring—diversions beyond a few distractions like playing golf, sipping Jameson, or puffing on cigars. As colleague and client needs for me faded, my writing and mentoring filled a creative void I sorely needed. To successfully navigate the changes, you must find diversions and start working on them well in advance.

Next, I deal with embracing reality when you no longer add value and need to move on.

The End of Adding Value

"If your presence doesn't add value, your absence won't make a difference."—Zero Dean, Writer

I was privileged to represent Edward Jay Phillips, the son of advice columnist Abigail Van Buren ("Dear Abby"). While best known for his career in the distilled spirits business, he was an inspirational entrepreneur and philanthropist. His word was his bond. He died too young, as many great people do, and I miss his wisdom.

As he and I walked one night in Paris where we were making a deal to sell a large part of his business, I commented on how well I thought the negotiations were going with the other side. He remarked, "Don't judge a man by the promises he makes, but by the footsteps he leaves." He was right. The other side of that deal made promises they eventually never kept—nor, in hindsight, do I think they ever intended to. While Eddie made hundreds of millions in the sale, it seemed he was selling too soon. His profits were rising and the reputation for the products was consistently growing. I asked him why he wanted to sell at a time that I thought was premature. In a classic Eddie Phillips philosophical response, he answered, "Doug, once you get to a point where you feel in your heart that you're not adding value to an enterprise when others could do better, you need to leave." I took that to heart. So should you. When you know your heart no longer wants the daily grind, you must change the model or move on.

In the years since Eddie and I had that walk, I appreciate that adding value is a two-way street. In my case, I was adding value throughout the years I actively practiced. Heeding Eddie's words, I realized in 2018 that others, many of whom I mentored, could add more value and that moving on to new ventures before my contributions ebbed was the right thing to do.

The End of Adding Value

I could have stayed and done fine for myself, but Eddie would have asked, "Is that what's best for the enterprise?" The answer was obviously "*no.*" I believed that opportunity lay ahead in finding how to add value to the firm in different ways, which was what my 2021, 2022, 2023, and 2024 proposals were all about. I outlined how I could continue to add value through mentoring, marketing, and, perhaps, charting how to deal with other senior partners facing, but not embracing, transition. For that to work, the firm needed to believe in the same values. Apart from addressing the needs of other senior partners, the firm saw value in my contributions through 2023, but never addressed them in detail—nor were they willing to discuss a multi-year deal. Instead, the primary measure in my yearly deals from 2021 through 2023 was a combination of a modest draw and billable hours and collections. While the expected billable hours were modest, it was too high. As I noted in my 2022 proposal, my failure to meet the billable hour goal the firm established was likely because I had moved virtually all my clients with the specific intent of letting them go. I intentionally diminished demands for my time by letting others do the work. Any need for my involvement in legal advice for the clients I moved was increasingly limited. In addition, my billing rate was high, and clients often balked at it. However, I doubt I would have billed much more if the rate was lower. In a successful plan, billable hours are not a measure of adding value and never should be. The firm could not get its head around that reality.

The proper measure is whether I added value in other ways that justified my compensation. I think I did.

When it came to negotiating my deal for 2023, I again submitted a plan. Regrettably, it was ignored and replaced with a commission deal. I got a percentage of collections on my hours and on matters where I had some portion of the origination credits. There was no acknowledgment of value for my contributions to mentoring, marketing, or transitioning. I was a salesperson. From the firm's perspective, that was a fine approach. Focus on the bottom line is always the priority of any profit-making business.

I accepted the deal, but to properly plan my future and my own "bottom line," I decided that my employee relationship with the firm would not go beyond 2023. Instead, I proposed a consultant agreement for 2024, continuing to mentor young lawyers on business development.

Ironically, in July 2023, I was mistakenly cc'd on an email that made it clear some in the firm were not interested in any working affiliation in 2024. It was apparent my fan club was shrinking! Of course, that disappointed me, but I chose not to be angry with them or myself. Just saddened by how short-sighted some of the firm's leadership could be in mentoring and dealing with senior lawyers. But they were not alone in that. Law firms do not invest in seniors. Or, on a more personal level, the importance of me as a mentor to young attorneys.

I submitted my proposal for 2024 in July 2023. The firm finally responded in October, rejecting most of my proposal and countering with a limited consulting agreement. I agreed to the deal. I am not suggesting the firm treated me poorly. I was just disappointed.

However, the firm and I agreed that there would be no relationship beyond 2024.

So, in January 2024, I announced the opening of the Law Offices of Douglas J. Wood. From Big Law to Solo. Of course, I have a detailed written plan. Time will tell how it works out, but it's exciting.

Which brings me to respect.

Respect

"Only when the last tree has died and the last river has been poisoned and the last fish been caught will we realize we cannot eat money."—Cree Indian Proverb

In a law firm, your compensation is a large measure of the professional respect the firm holds for you, but the money is only part of the equation. Being appreciated in other ways is as equally important as your compensation.

Nothing is more important than feeling respected; what you say is worth listening to and your contributions are appreciated. Those intangibles become more important when moving an active practice to others as compensation naturally declines. Preventing respect from following a similar downward path is a challenge.

The process reminds me of how some cultures see the value of elders. The Greeks and Romans of centuries past had societies that depended upon their elders for guidance and inspiration. Most modern society does not do so. One exception in the United States is the culture of Native Americans. It remains rooted in their past. Elders among them remain essential in their society, sitting on top of the family hierarchy. Today, there are over 500 Native American nations. While attitudes differ among those nations, respecting elders' wisdom and life experiences is universal. Young Native Americans make a concerted effort to include their elders in decisions. They may decide to go in a different direction, but they listen.

It does not take a lot to let someone know you appreciate everything they did in the past. Indeed, you may learn something from them. For Native Americans, this interaction results in the elders passing on their wisdom to younger members of the nation. In most societies today, that is a goal neither encouraged nor appreciated. The business community, including law firms, could learn much from the Greeks, Romans, and Native

Americans. Ask yourself, how many elders does your firm respect and make part of the decision process? I doubt you'll need your second hand to count them.

Today, I devote much of my time to giving presentations on one-on-one mentoring of other attorneys and business development projects I help generate. I also occasionally teach business development to lawyers in bigger groups who want to learn why planning is the best road to success. Some of the equity partners in Reed Smith today are "graduates" of my approach. I take great pride in their success, but most of all, I like to work with other attorneys, moving their practices. That never happened at Reed Smith and I've realized it is largely a fiction elsewhere. That is indeed a pity.

I knew my compensation would fall when I lost equity status. That made sense. My only question was whether the firm believed there were other ways my contributions warranted the compensation I felt I deserved. To be honest, I battle with being too sensitive when I am ignored or when I read an email where the writer notes they're moving me to bcc, so I am no longer involved in future email exchanges. To this day, I battle against developing a thin skin and overreacting. When I did (as I still do), I reminded myself of a quote from Konrad Adenauer: "A thick skin is a gift from God."

Next, I'll talk about leadership and its importance during the journey.

Leadership

"A true leader has the confidence to stand alone, the courage to make tough decisions, and the compassion to listen to the needs of others. He does not set out to be a leader, but becomes one by the equality of his actions and the integrity of his intent."
—*General Douglas MacArthur*

Having run a law firm for over a decade, I can assure readers that few places are as lonely as leadership. Harry Truman's expression that the "buck stops here" is as true today as it was when he faced the horrific decision he had to make to end World War II. While I do not mean to suggest any decisions I made in leading a law firm compared to his challenges, the fate and future of the people you lead falls on your shoulders. That can be a heavy burden.

Leaders must be decisive and often decide on too few facts. They usually go with their gut. When they are wrong, they decide how to correct those mistakes, often at their own sacrifice. While being the big dog certainly has its benefits—"If you ain't the lead dog, the scenery never changes"—it is sometimes necessary to marginalize a few for the better of the whole. I know the firm's decision to support my plan's novelty was challenging to accept, and I appreciate their courage in doing so. I was disappointed, however, over what I perceived as marginalization and ignoring my contributions or, admittedly, putting my ego on my sleeve, not being told by management that they appreciated me.

I understood the firm had to deal with the economics of my deal. They could not pay others the rewards of taking over my clients and simultaneously compensate me for the practice I built. There had to be give and take. While I hoped in 2020 that the firm would give me a multi-year deal and pay me the amount I proposed after moving millions to others, it was not in the cards. Despite being complex, my plan would have incentivized me and those to whom I delegated clients. It was ignored, but that's okay. Everyone thinks they are smarter than they really are (including me) and that what they say should be taken as Gospel. I am no exception. Ultimately, what the firm paid me was fair, and while it had little to incentivize me, I can't complain. The lesson for readers is not to get too caught up in yourself. You're not that important.

Which brings me to transparency.

Transparency

"Life is filigree work. What is written clearly is not worth much, it's the transparency that counts."—Louis-Ferdinand Celine, French Novelist

Being tactful is hard. On the one hand, you want to make sure a person understands your point. On the other hand, you cannot berate or bully someone and have any chance of seeing him or her go in the direction you want. If you are unclear in what you mean, you cannot criticize someone else for misunderstanding.

The only way to ensure you communicate your message is to be transparent about what you want to accomplish, why you are taking the tact you are, how you expect others to take part, and what a person involved can expect as an outcome. Likewise, the other person needs to be transparent in their ability to achieve what they are asked to do. Anything less than a balance of mutual transparency will inevitably lead to negative consequences for everyone involved. With good intentions, lawyers like to say, "Put it in writing." That is a good idea. After all, few people are left, like Frankie Valle, the legendary Four Seasons lead singer, who often honor commitments throughout a career with a handshake rather than a written contract. (I was privileged to have known him and to see such integrity firsthand.)

When I proposed my plan, I considered transparency a key to its success. Everyone needed to know what I expected of him or her and what he or she could expect from me. The written plan set that out well. I hoped that through transparency, those involved at every level would trust my judgment and willingly want to participate in the process. I was also transparent that participation by anyone in transferring my clients required that they adopt their own written business plan on how they would build the relationship beyond what I had accomplished. I was giving people an opportunity afforded to few—a lead position in marshaling millions of dollars of business.

Those on my original plan opened their arms to the process, with few exceptions. Those who did not were not part of it. They made that decision with open eyes. That was fine. Some had their own views of building their practices, and taking control of one or more of my clients was not as promising as they had seen their own business development efforts would be. I had no problem with that and did not criticize anyone who chose a different way. But without question, those who worked with me knew what I expected of them and what they could expect from me.

That meant they needed to be honest with me. Their best approach was to read, listen, respond to what I had to say, and understand my motivations behind it. That is why I set forth a specific timetable to execute the plan and suggestions on what I expected post-execution. It is why I consistently had meetings to discuss what needed to be done.

In the almost three years during which I implemented the plan, I was pleased with the progress and the commitment of those who took part. Colleagues to whom I transferred clients met with me frequently, and we had honest discussions of the challenges they faced and how I could help them. We still do this. I still ghostwrite emails for them to send. I think they all understand that I want them to succeed and that I'm not just going off into the sunset, leaving them with the burdens. Selfishly, I want to leave a legacy of generosity and support (that ego thing again).

I had seen the opposite at Hall Dickler when a senior partner, Gerry Dickler, retired and demanded a deal that included overly generous compensation for what he had done in the past with no contributions to the future. He got his deal because he threatened to take the firm's biggest client to somewhere else if Hall Dickler did not agree to his demands. I was not on the executive committee but would have probably made the same decision since he had all the leverage. It left a sour taste in my mouth, particularly when I tried to renegotiate his deal when I took over the firm's leadership. He essentially told me to go f*ck myself. Years later, I saw Gerry sitting alone in an expensive restaurant. I asked the server if he came to the restaurant often and was told he did at least a couple of days a week. When I asked if anyone ever joined him, I was told no. He always ate alone. I do not know if he saw me, and I certainly did not go over and say hello. Karma is a bitch.

To be honest, I was disappointed by how the firm handled the initial stages of the post-transition years. It lacked transparency in the sense I hoped I would see. I had only brief communications in response to the specifics of what I asked for in a March 2020 proposal for 2021. It was an offer I thought through carefully and consulted with others to be sure I was being reasonable. Based upon their advice, it grew into something I considered helpful for the firm and motivational for me.

Unfortunately, the pandemic hit, and the firm understandably needed to attend to things far more important than my deal, so I chose not to press the issue. That may have been a mistake because on December 31, 2020, my last day of equity partner status, I had no deal for 2021. I did not know what was going to happen on January 1. While I assumed I remained some sort of employee and that I would have the title of partner or counsel, I did not know what the firm would pay me or any details of what else was involved. I had not been an employee of any organization since I became an equity partner in Hall Dickler in the early '80s.

We had to negotiate a deal in precious little time. The result was an approach that largely ignored my March 2020 proposal and began with two forms, one with the title "Senior Partner" and the other with "Senior Counsel." Both were poorly drafted and filled with typos. It was unclear how old these two forms were, but they appeared hastily put together with inconsistencies—nothing major, but inconsistent. To the firm's credit, it corrected everything once I pointed out the errors, but I realized what I proposed in March 2020 was simply no longer on the table. I doubt it ever was. What was missing was a robust discussion of my March 2020 proposal, why I asked what I asked for, and what the firm could expect. My 2021 arrangement was a form.

The firm followed the same approach in 2022, 2023, and 2024, mainly ignoring my proposals, emphasizing reducing compensation, and pushing for more client transition. I understand and appreciate that the firm may have been losing patience with me, but I believe ignoring my proposals over the years was a genuine loss for the firm.

Next, I'll talk about a lesson this taught me and how they might provide some valuable lessons.

A Lesson Not Learned

"Remember one thing, son. People are no damn good."
—*Col. Gilbert F. Wood (Ret.)*

When I was ten years old, my dad gave me that advice. We were walking down a street in San Francisco the day before his formal retirement took place at the Presidio. He suddenly stopped, looked down at me and said those nine words I'll never forget. I can remember asking myself if he was serious. As I look back on his life, he probably was. He served in two wars and saw things as evil as humankind can make them. Baby Boomers may never fully appreciate the sacrifices he and others in his generation made for all of us, even less so for generations that have followed. It is a pity our safety and freedom came at such a price for them.

If someone asked me to give similar advice to my children, I would tell them people are good, and if you believe in them, they will believe in you. Of course, there will always be some who would not hesitate to stick a knife in your back (or worse) if it was to their advantage. Some people have certainly tried to do so with me. But you should be fine if you find time to identify and avoid them.

During my transition, I can honestly say everyone meant well. They may not have been as responsive as I would have liked or as impressed with me as I was about myself (that damned ego thing again), but I never doubted their compassion. I cannot imagine moving in an environment of distrust and greed. Sadly, I suspect that's the norm at many law firms, and I am one of the lucky few. I also like to think my choices influenced my luck. I choose not to be surrounded by jerks. While there were some exceptions to that rule over the last forty-five years, including at Reed Smith, there have been very few.

That said, I would fool myself if I didn't acknowledge that there are many people in this world, as my father said, who are no damn good. I was lucky not to encounter too many of them in my career. Be ready for it, but do not let it derail your plan. Adjust. Remember two critical pieces of advice from Niccolo Machiavelli: "Keep your friends close and your enemies closer," and "Never do your enemy a minor injury."

Next, I'll address relaxing despite the storms that might surround you.

Relaxing

"Tension is who you think you should be. Relaxation is who you are."
—*Chinese Proverb*

Finding time to relax is a far more significant challenge than I initially believed. Lawyers rarely know how to relax. Their obsession with servicing clients and solving complex problems keeps their minds in high gear. I can only imagine it is worse for healthcare professionals. They make decisions that can mean the difference between life and death. Decisions by lawyers (except criminal defense lawyers) primarily affect only finances and family cohesion. Nonetheless, your daily practice demands are always on your mind and thwart relaxing efforts.

I had my diversions—writing, golf, Jameson, and good cigars—but relaxing proved elusive. Even getting a good night's sleep became difficult, with my mind constantly thinking about the unfamiliar changes and challenges I faced and their impact on my family and myself.

I dealt with it through meditation, mainly as I lay in bed trying to fall asleep. There are many programs on meditation in the market. Yes, "there's an app for that."

Sarah Stuart, a former client turned meditation guru, taught me the technique that helps me sleep—progressive relaxation. It is simple. I start by focusing on relaxing on my toes and work my way up the body, part by part—feet, shins, calves, etc. Whenever I have done so, I have never made it past my chest before I fall asleep. I just have to be patient and not rush it. It is amazing how concentrating on relaxing pushes your worries, fears, anxieties, painful memories, and other thoughts out of your mind.

Other forms of meditation, not intended to cause you to fall asleep, free your mind of distracting thoughts. Regardless, meditation works by relaxing you and calming your nerves, at least for a while.

So be open-minded to meditation.

And, as I'll cover next, deciding what not to do.

Do Not Do List

"Never attempt to teach a pig to sing; it wastes your time and annoys the pig."—Robert Heinlein, Science Fiction Writer

Here is an idea you should try.

Rather than create a to-do list, create a do-not-do list. Mine is pretty simple:

- Do not deal with those who aggravate me.
- Do not argue with people who do not listen to me.
- Do not work more than an hour without a break.
- Do not read or watch the news for more than an hour a day. It is too dominated by negative reporting and falsehoods.
- Do not eat anything you don't like. No matter how you prepare them, they are still Brussels sprouts.
- Do not let a bad golf score spoil my mood. It is only a game that I will never be good at playing.
- Do not deny myself something if I really want it. Life is too short.

What is on your Do Not Do List?

Next, I move on to improvements that could have been made.

Improvement

"Everything is perfect and there is always room for improvement."
—*Shunryū Suzuki, Zen Monk*

If I were doing this again, would I have changed anything? Absolutely. Suzuki said that while things may be perfect, they can always be improved.

More frequent communications with firm management would have been an improvement. As I mentioned earlier, feeling respected is essential in achieving goals. It is what motivates someone. But everyone's schedules are tight and running a billion-dollar law firm leaves little room for smaller projects like a partner moving a practice, even if it is worth millions. The only way to do that is to ensure you have calls scheduled on the calendar and do not have sporadic communications when facing an issue or challenge. The expression, "Out of sight, out of mind" is very real. Not that management did not appreciate what I was doing; it was that they did not know how much I was doing. It is flattering that they trusted me, but more feedback and dialog would have been helpful. That failure falls on me. I should have pushed harder to be on their agenda.

The second improvement stems from the first. Had we talked more, management would have better understood what I wanted long-term and the value I thought I could add. Rather than leaving them speculating, I would have been very specific. Had such conversations occurred, I believe the negotiations of my arrangements over the past few years would have been smoother and probably more beneficial to the firm and lucrative for me. Instead, the pandemic interrupted communications in 2020, as the firm faced more significant issues. The 2021 deal wasn't completed until well into January of that year. While we were able to complete subsequent deals by December of each year, the deals were slightly modified versions of the form used in 2021. There was no excuse for leaving me hanging for so long. On that, the fault lies with the firm.

Improvement

A third improvement addresses the first two—formalizing the process. A more formal process would have allowed everyone to map out the program efficiently. It would have humanized it. While I provided periodic updates, I got little feedback in return. It was not until I gave the firm the list of partners to whom lead attorney status was assigned that the firm took a keener interest. The partners then approving my recommendations disagreed with some of my choices, primarily based upon their review of who had recorded the most billable hours with a client in the past year. They missed the point. Client relationships are not dependent upon who bills the most hours. It got a little tense until my practice group leader stepped in and insisted the firm accept my decisions. In the end, he and I prevailed. That last-minute tension could have been avoided if the process had been more formalized.

Last, the firm could have done a much better job involving me in decisions that potentially negatively affected the clients I moved. This usually happened when another lawyer not associated with one of my clients brought in adverse work that might raise a conflict issue. Once I broke up my business, the "clout" of each of those to whom a client was transferred was not as significant as mine was when I controlled all the clients. I saw decisions being made for financial purposes that troubled me from conflict management practices. But Big Law understandably focuses on revenue to support the massive organizations such firms have become. They seek conflict waivers, all within the confines of legal ethics, but sometimes, they also pose unsettling business conflicts. So, while it disappointed me not to be a part of the decision-making process, I was not surprised. I just expected more from some of my former colleagues.

Most of all, nothing in the process dealt with the emotional side of transitioning. I felt a bit lost. Whether or not it was reality, I perceived my communications were being ignored or becoming marginalized. I do not mean to imply any of this was intentional. I understand leadership in an institution as large and complex as Reed Smith and other similarly sized organizations demands attention to far more important things, but something of minor importance in the big scheme to the firm can be paramount to an individual. It seemed I needed to reach out for input on multiple occasions for the same issues. While this may have been more perception than reality, it was unsettling. I never doubted the firm's integrity or believed management did not care. But getting only one phone call from the former Global Managing Partner and never a call from the current Global Managing Partner in the last three years hurt. Perhaps they assumed I was tough enough to deal with it. At the beginning of the planning, I thought I was. That became more difficult as December 31, 2023, loomed closer. In February 2024, however, I received a lovely bottle of Lanson Champagne with my name and photograph etched on the bottle and a tag on the net thanking me and wishing me luck. That was a nice gesture. But regardless, firms need to apply more TLC to make the process welcoming and comfortable. Those readers who are in firm management should take that observation to heart. When one suddenly feels they are becoming a commodity, it is a bitter pill.

The solution is a process that addresses both the financial and emotional challenges and creates a defined program that benefits both the firm and the individual.

The first step is to establish cohorts of those in similar situations. In that respect, a group called The Elders inspired me. Founded in 2007 by Nelson Mandela with the urging of performer Peter Gabriel and entrepreneur Richard Branson, its members are leading politicians who are no longer in office. Gabriel commented on its formation: "In traditional societies, elders always had a role in conflict resolution, long-term thinking and applying wisdom wherever it was needed." Why shouldn't a law firm, particularly one with an aging population, take a similar approach?

In 2021, I proposed that Reed Smith add a new cohort to those on its roster. Given Reed Smith's propensity to use titles with "RS" in them, it was natural to call it "EldeRS." I suggested we set aside a budget to support the effort and that a member of EldeRS should be part of the senior management team dedicated to older partners. EldeRS could provide a think tank environment for sage advice on issues facing the firm. While a firm's future is in the junior associates and partners rising to the top, the shared experiences of those who succeeded in the past should make the journey of those younger ones easier and more profitable. A win-win. While the firm never entertained my idea of the EldeRS, I am hopeful it will someday be embraced and funded, but I won't hold my breath. I don't know of a single law firm with such a program.

Another step is to retain professionals to assist where needed, more than just bankers, insurance agents, estate planning experts, and elder care consultants. None of them addresses the psychological side. Most are about what you are eventually leaving to others—directly and indirectly telling you to "get your affairs in order," like a doctor giving you a diagnosis of a terminal illness. The centerpiece should not be the negative. It should be the positive of what you can do to remain active in the profession you pursued for decades and, perhaps, for a decade or two longer. While much of what Reed Smith's management did was positive, their priorities in dealing with transitioning partners were lacking. That said, my guess is that it's the same or worse at other firms.

Appendix H includes a list of things firms can consider in developing programs supporting senior attorneys' transition.

That brings me back to my father. When he retired in 1960, the Army had a beautiful ceremony for him and about a dozen others who were also retiring. I'll never forget it and the pride my father felt. A simple gesture. Law firms should learn from that.

What is Good for the Goose . . .

"People should decide what success means for them, and not be distracted by accepting others' definitions of success."—Tony Levin, Musician

One of the difficult things to accept is that others to whom I delegated a client did not see servicing the client in the same way I did. I had to realize they had different priorities and were comfortable with other things.

They had other clients, some of whom were very important—perhaps more important than the clients I delegated to them. Understanding that proved difficult and frustrating. At times, I thought of taking the client back, although I knew that was not practical, nor was it what I wanted to do.

It was most frustrating when they ignored my suggestions on how to market or approached my ideas half-heartedly. If there is one thing I know I am good at, it is marketing to clients. I constantly sought opportunities to reach out to existing and prospective clients, often combing the trade press and online news. I passed these ideas on. While some folks on the team followed the advice, others did not. I thought they were missing chances to build their business. I realized, however, that some folks are uncomfortable with marketing. Some hit a wall when they needed to go over it and ask the client or prospect for work, or they marketed differently than I did. Opportunities were lost, but I accepted my model was not the only one that worked.

Initially, I would send reminders of what needed to be done. Eventually, I did it less and less to avoid getting frustrated. I had to accept that their approach differed from mine. That didn't make what they did wrong; it was just different.

Ultimately, the litmus test was how they performed with the combination of their clients and the ones I delegated to them. On that, they all did great. I learned that whatever recipe I had for my success was not

What is Good for the Goose . . .

necessarily theirs. As long as one follows business fundamentals, the variations on how to succeed are endless. Their performances prove that.

Part of giving business to others is letting go of it and accepting the program. It is much easier to do so if it is your program and not one dictated by someone else.

Support

"The love of family and the admiration of friends are much more important than wealth and privilege."—Charles Kuralt

Above all else, the support of family and friends is a critical element to a successful transition. Logically, I received support from the firm and my colleagues—they all had a self-interest at heart and understandably so—but the support I got from my wife, family, and friends was most important and comforting. My support group is second to none.

In 2023, my wife, Carol Ann, and I celebrated our fiftieth anniversary. She has seen all my ups and downs throughout my career. She has been my greatest fan and my harshest critic. She has been my friend and partner and, occasionally, my antagonist. Our love for one another has stood every test of time. While she had many questions (and still does) as I moved through the process, she had my back throughout the journey. When I needed encouragement, she was there. When I needed suggestions, she offered them. Sometimes even when I did not want to hear them. And when I needed to be left alone with no suggestions, she understood—usually.

As Jerry Seinfeld, one of our favorite comedians, once said, "There is no such thing as fun for the whole family." Carol Ann felt much of the same anxiety I was feeling. Without her support, success in the process would have been impossible and the burdens unbearable.

I have three terrific children—Joshua, Meghan, and Andrea—all of whom are successful. I also have two wonderful in-laws—Bianca and Scott—who were wise enough to marry Joshua and Andrea, respectively. I also have five beautiful grandchildren—Sienna, Sydney, Skye, Everett, and Landon. Visiting with them and occasionally talking to them about how my life is changing makes the process easier and more enjoyable. While my grandchildren do not know what this is about, they smile anyway. That is all I need.

Support

I am also lucky to have an older brother, Gil, and an older sister, Martha, with whom I talk now and then. They are great supporters who are wiser than me. It is ironic. I went from an annoying little brother in childhood whom they took glee in tormenting to that sibling they now nurture in their own ways. I depend upon them and their wisdom.

I also depended upon Nancy Schulein, my executive assistant for over twenty-five years. She stayed on top of what I needed to do and when it needed to be done. I miss her terribly now that I'm no longer with the firm. She was a great sounding board for what was happening at the firm that I overlooked (or forgot). She was beloved by clients, maybe even more than I was!

Finally, I am blessed with a group of friends I have known since fifth grade. Nine of us are still in touch. I talk to some of them every day. We all text one another with random observations and thoughts, some as politically incorrect as they can get and others more insightful than you will get from any of the great philosophers. We go on trips together. We are inseparable. Having known one another for so long means we have no secrets or competition. We are friends just for the pleasure of being friends. With that came group support whenever I needed it.

And I'm making new friends here in North Carolina.

Be sure to set up your own support groups. You will need them.

Let's get to the bottom line.

The Bottom Line

"The bottom line is to have fun and enjoy life."
—Rekha (Bhanurekha Ganesan), *Hindi Film Actress*

In the end, it's all about enjoying your life. To do that while you're winding down your business or transitioning to retirement, remember these ten rules:

1. Choose your timing. Don't let others do it for you.
2. Accept the reality of irrelevancy. It happens to all of us.
3. Adopt a written plan founded in transparency.
4. Trust others. That's the only way it will work.
5. Find diversions to take your mind off the change and reduce your stress.
6. Stay positive and suppress your anger. Negativity and anger will only make the transition harder.
7. Keep a sense of humor. If you don't have one, watch and listen to someone who does and who makes you laugh.
8. Prepare your "Do Not Do" list.
9. Block out any jerks around you. You can't change them at this point in life, so don't try. They're just unnecessary interruptions.
10. Above all else, develop a support group with whom you can be open and honest. Talk to them often. You cannot succeed if you try to do it alone.

And now, my final word.

The Final Word

"In three words, I can sum up everything I've learned about life: It goes on."—Robert Frost

Robert Frost could not have said it better. We cannot stop time, but we can influence what we do with that time and where we go with our lives.

Some suggest I was crazy giving away millions in business, knowing that my compensation would suffer or the plan might hasten my departure from the firm. Those quick to that opinion were, of course, right to a degree, but for me, I predicated my decision on my desire not to, literally or figuratively, die at my desk. I have seen too many colleagues over my career who held on too long.

So, I controlled my destiny as best I could rather than have it controlled by others. In addition, I am still healthy and excited to continue working, particularly since I am admitted to the North Carolina bar where I now make my home. I stayed with Reed Smith for as long as I felt I added value, and the firm thought I contributed meaningfully. We ended the relationship amicably.

I realized this in mid-2022 when I told the managing partner I thought I was overpaid for the first time in my career. I believe the statement shocked him. I explained I had too much time on my hands and wanted to do more, feeling underutilized. Being underutilized is not something I want to feel. No one does. He never called me back.

I now have a new Strategic Business Plan with a SWOT analysis, goals, and tactics necessary to succeed. I'm excited because I'll be doing what I love the most: helping young lawyers succeed. To that, I've now added helping older lawyers let go. And now and again, I continue to provide legal advice to special people in my life. I couldn't ask for more success. But I have been doing this kind of planning for nearly fifty years. A piece of cake. I hope you try it, too.

Because in the end, others may decide you are irrelevant. That doesn't matter. All that matters is how relevant you feel.

As a Life and Leadership Coach, Tim Austin, put it, "Whether transition is forced upon us or comes about by personal choice, making it to the other side requires that we intentionally process the loss, celebrate the victories, and plan for the next productive season."

So, if you see me eating alone in a restaurant, come on over and say hi. I'll buy you a drink.

Appendix A:

SWOT Analysis Worksheet

Step One

Strengths	Weaknesses
- In what skill sets do you excel? - What are your competitive advantages? - What are your strongest client relationships? - What unique resources can you draw upon, personal and professional? - What do others see as your strengths? - What advantages do you have that others don't have (for example, certifications, education, or connections)? - What do you do better than anyone else? - Which of your achievements are you most proud of? - What values do you believe in that others fail to exhibit? - Are you part of a network that no one else is involved in? - What connections do you have with influential people?	- What could you improve? - What are the gaps in your practice expertise? - Where do you have fewer resources than others? - What are others likely to see as your weaknesses? - What damage did the COVID pandemic have on your practice? - What tasks do you usually avoid because you don't feel confident doing them? - Are you completely confident in your education and skills training? If not, where are you weakest? - What are your negative work habits (for example, are you often late, disorganized, have a short temper, or are poor at handling stress)? - Do you have personality traits that hold you back in your

• Others?	field? For instance, a fear of public speaking would be a major weakness if you have to conduct meetings regularly. • Is there a need in your practice area that no one in the firm is handling? • Others?
Opportunities • What opportunities are open to you? • What clients offer you significant growth opportunities? • What trends could you take advantage of? • How can you turn your strengths into opportunities? • Are there opportunities post-COVID? • What new technology can help you? Can you get help from others or from people via the Internet? • Is your practice sector growing? If so, how can you take advantage of the current market? • Do you have a network of strategic contacts to help you or offer sound advice?	**Threats** • What threats could harm you? • What is your competition doing? • What threats do your weaknesses expose you to? • What external pressures—economic and regulatory—may threaten growth? • What obstacles do you currently face at work? • Are any of your colleagues competing with you for projects or roles? • Is your job (or the demand for what you do) changing? • Does changing technology threaten your position? • Could any of your weaknesses lead to threats? • Others?

Appendix A:

- What trends (management or otherwise) do you see in the firm, and how can you take advantage of them? - Are any of your competitors failing to do something important? If so, can you take advantage of their mistakes? - If a colleague is on an extended leave, could you take on some of this person's projects to gain experience? - Others?	

Now fill in your SWOT analysis (add rows as necessary).
BE HONEST!

Strengths:

Weaknesses:

Opportunities:

Appendix A:

Threats:

Step Two

Strategic Goals for the Current Year

Building on your SWOT Analysis, list your strategic goals that are a combination of attainable and a reasonable stretch. Strategic goals are what you want to accomplish for yourself to make you a better lawyer and business producer.

Strategic Goals:

1.
2.
3.
4.
5.

Step Three

Tactics to Achieve Goals:

For each goal, list:

- **What** are you going to do? Be specific. For example, "Reach out to client" is NOT a tactic. "Reach out to John Smith at client and invite him to [fill in the event]" is a tactic.
- **When** are you going to do it? If you don't attach a date, it won't

happen.

- **How** are you going to do it? While emailing is an option, it is too cluttered. Consider calling or trying old school, e.g., a letter or personal note.
- **Who** do you need to help you execute the tactic, what do you want them to do, and when do you want them to do it? You don't have to do this alone. Recruit others to help, e.g., your executive assistant or folks in business development.
- **Why** will your tactic help you achieve the goal?—Explain why the tactic will help achieve your goal. This may seem obvious, but stating it reinforces your focus.
- Your list should have multiple tactics for each goal. The more tactics for each goal, the greater your odds of succeeding. Remember, tactics are focused and specific, not vague ideas.

Goal [Restate the Goal]	Tactics
What are you going to do?	
How are you going to do it?	
When are you going to do it?	
Who do you need to help you execute the tactic, what do you want them to do, and when do you want them to do it?	
Why will your tactic help you achieve the goal?	

Appendix A:

No format is right or wrong. The best is whatever works for you. Here's another approach:

What are you going to do?	When are you going to do it?	How are you going to do it?
[tactic]	[on what specific day will you begin or do it?]	[how—who do you need to help you, will you meet personally, will you email, etc.?]
[tactic]	[on what specific day will you begin or do it?]	[how—who do you need to help you, will you meet personally, will you email, etc.?]

Steps Four

Schedule for Reviews and Revisions to Plan

Set calendar review sessions where you will review the Plan with your EA or someone else who will help keep you on schedule. Do this once a month. This is a critical step to success as it reinforces the plan and best ensures success. Where appropriate, add notes from each session and revise your plan accordingly.

Date	Time	Attendee(s)	Notes
January x			
February x			
Etc. for next 12 months			

Step Five

Build and Use Networks

One method to build your network using Outlook. You may use others. Regardless, keep adding contacts as you develop more extensive networks.

To the extent possible, record their names, addresses, emails, phones, etc. and add labels for their category, e.g., clients, prospective clients, friends, industry, etc. You can create as many categories as you'd like from the Categorize pull-down menu in the Outlook Contact file. If you know anything about them personally, enter it into the Notes section.

Establish email mailing lists:

- Open the Address Book function on Outlook email header bar.
- Click on File.
- Click on New Entry.
- Click on New Contact Group.
- Give the Group a Name, e.g., "Network Friends."
- Click on Add Members.
- Click on "From Outlook Contacts" if you want to add someone outside the firm.
- Click on "From Address Book" if you want to add someone from within the firm.
- Scroll to the contact and add them as a "Member."

CAUTION: When using your email lists, you generally want to put the network members on the bcc line so they don't appear in the email addresses. You can do this by emailing yourself in the "To" line and everyone from the network in the "bcc" line.

Appendix A:

Step Six

Grade Yourself

The easiest way to grade yourself is to make notes on the plan, or you can highlight those goals and tactics that worked and those that did not, e.g., red highlight for where you missed and green where you succeeded. Then use the results to help build your plan for the following year. For example, if you missed a goal or tactic, how can you better ensure you can accomplish it in the future? What can you change, or should you eliminate it and move on to something else? For those you accomplished, plan what you do next to build on the success.

Step Seven

Repeat

Do it all over again, starting with a new SWOT analysis for the new year.

Appendix B

Jeffrey Lant Seven Contact Matrix

List the key prospects in your plan. Fill in brief details in each contact box, e.g., date, event, etc. The details need not be specific. The point is to ensure that by year's end, all contact boxes for a prospect have been filled in.

Prospect Name	Contact 1	Contact 2	Contact 3	Contact 4	Contact 5	Contact 5	Contact 7

Appendix C

Tactics

Building a successful law practice requires strategic planning and effective tactics. Here are some basic tactics to consider:

- Identify legal conferences, seminars, and networking events to connect with other professionals in the field where decision makers will be among attendees or who are speakers you want to meet. Map out a plan on how you'll get to meet them. Follow up after their presentation with a handwritten note on how you enjoyed their talk.

- Join local bar associations or legal organizations to expand your network, but make sure their members are movers and shakers. Focus on smaller committees that concentrate in your practice area. It's not just about joining; it's about joining strategically.

- Build a list of potential mentors—lawyers inside and outside your firm and successful business managers. Think about what you want in a mentor. See below for more on choosing the right mentors. Set up a schedule to reach out to them. Appendix D lists attributes you'll want to consider in picking mentors.

- Set up time each day or week to review professional social media platforms like LinkedIn to connect with potential clients and colleagues. *Never* post a like. It's a waste of time. *Always* post a comment. Get into the conversation.

- Cultivate relationships with other professionals who can refer clients, such as accountants, financial advisors, and consultants. Make a list and set up meetings with each.

- Join referral networks or establish reciprocal referral relationships with trusted lawyers. When you make a referral, be clear you expect reciprocity. When you get a referral, refer something to them at your next opportunity. If the referral is due to a conflict, never poach the client for work other than what was referred to you. Refer them to their established counsel if the referral asks for additional work.

- Set a written schedule to attend community events and engage in community service to network with potential clients and referral sources.

- Identify your niche and develop specialized knowledge within a specific area of the law. Ask yourself what's on the horizon that in-house counsel may worry about. Write a white paper and post it on social media or as a firm bulletin. Execute a thought leadership strategy by regularly publishing informative articles, blog posts, or videos on legal topics. Identify underserved or emerging markets within the legal industry, such as the gig economy, esports, or sustainable businesses, and position yourself as an expert. Show you're thinking about the future.

- Continuously stay updated with the latest legal developments and industry trends. Obviously? Yes, but do you read the trade press? Do you have notifications set up on Google or other reporting services? If all you're doing is keeping up on legal developments, you're dealing in the past. Non-legal publications are better predictors of the future.

- Consider pursuing additional certifications or advanced degrees in your chosen field to enhance credibility. While this can be expensive, adding to your resume with additional certifications or degrees sets you apart from most competitors and adds to your brand.

- Take part in continuing legal education courses and workshops as a speaker. When attending to earn CLE credits, consider courses outside your practice area but covered by your firm so you can identify issues should you be conversing with a potential client with interests in those areas. With even a little knowledge, you can have an intelligent conversation leading to a referral.

- Explore partnerships with professionals who cater to the same

Appendix C

- client base but offer non-legal services, such as financial planners or business consultants. Identify the conferences they go to and consider attending. Don't limit your conferences to groups that your competitors dominate. Organize joint seminars or webinars with non-lawyers to address legal and non-legal aspects of common client concerns, providing a holistic approach.

- Become conversant with artificial intelligence tools, such as chatbots or virtual assistants, to provide immediate responses to basic legal inquiries and improve client experience. Have conversations with the bots. It will surprise you how helpful those discussions can be.

- Devote at least 50 hours a year to pro bono services to marginalized communities or nonprofit organizations related to your chosen niche to gain exposure and contribute to a cause you care about.

- Establish how you're going to measure your success at year's end. Consider measuring the following, both objectively and subjectively.

- Client Satisfaction: Ask your clients for feedback at the conclusion of a matter or as a yearly review. They will appreciate the opportunity to tell you what you did right and give you advice on how to improve. In their companies, they likely go through the same review process and will react well to being asked to be the evaluator. This can lead to client testimonials and referrals and show that you are providing quality legal services and meeting, or better yet, exceeding their needs.

- Listings: Establish a reputation within the legal community and recognition from peers in legal directories and rankings.

- Professional Achievements: Your plan should have milestones you hope to achieve. List those where you succeeded and consider putting the failures in next year's plan or dropping them if you see they're unrealistic. Milestones must always be attainable. Some milestones are obvious, e.g., becoming a partner in a law firm, being appointed to a prestigious position, or winning a significant case.

Do you have any that are less obvious?

- Financial Performance: Financial success is often a metric used to measure success in any business, including law firms. Financial indicators can include revenue, profitability, and the ability to maintain a sustainable and thriving practice. See how you reached those milestones. Where you succeeded, make sure management knows. Where you failed, focus on tactics for the next year to succeed.
- Personal Fulfillment: Personal fulfillment and satisfaction can also measure success in your legal career. Assessing whether your work aligns with your values, interests, and long-term goals can be an essential measure of success. How is your work-life balance after a year of hard work on your plan? Did you live to work, or did you work to live? That's an important question.

Appendix D

Picking Mentors

A mentor should possess extensive experience and expertise in the legal field and other areas tangential to it, e.g., financial planning, M&A consulting, technology, etc., or mentors important in your personal life. You can undoubtedly make an extensive list of potential mentors inside and outside the legal profession. Once you have your list, rate your potential mentors on these attributes. They don't need to score high on every one of them. Remember, however, that simply because someone is successful does not mean they'll be an excellent mentor. In choosing mentors, you must pick people you think will succeed in that role. The last thing you want is to face a failed relationship. That hurts everyone. When choosing mentors, consider if they possess the following qualities and characteristics:

- Knowledge and deep understanding of the practice area or areas you are interested in and can provide valuable insights and guidance based on their own successful legal career.
- A good listener, able to understand your goals, concerns, and challenges.
- Able to communicate their advice, feedback, and knowledge in a clear and supportive manner.
- Available and committed to the mentoring relationship.
- Ascertain if they will invest their time and effort in providing guidance, answering questions, and offering support when needed.
- Shows high ethical standards and integrity and has a reputation for honesty, ethical behavior, and maintaining confidentiality. Trust is crucial in a mentoring relationship, as you will probably discuss confidential and sensitive matters.
- Can empathize with your experiences, offer encouragement during

difficult times, and provide guidance for overcoming obstacles.
- Has a strong network and can offer introductions, connections, and networking opportunities.
- Has values and promotes diversity and inclusion that support valuable insights and guidance on navigating these aspects of the profession. Look for someone who actively supports and encourages diversity and inclusion within the legal field.
- Someone you admire, respect, and like, with an emphasis on like. You need to feel comfortable with your mentors.

Appendix E

Understanding Your Numbers

Your business planning is ultimately directed toward advancing your career and compensation. Part of that process involves being promoted to the next tier of a firm's hierarchy. Besides executing your business plan, you must also pay attention to your numbers and reputation. If you have a plan, both are within your control.

Specific objective numbers measure attorney performance in a firm, all of which play a role in promotion and compensation. Understanding the terminology is essential. Here is an overview. Make sure you know how your firm views each.

- Billable Hours—The total hours you record that are billable to clients. Some firms allow non-billable hours to count towards billable hour targets, e.g., pro bono, CLE, committee work, etc. However, there is generally a cap on such hours, so while they may be necessary to your career experience, they have little impact on promotion or compensation.

- Working Attorney Receipts (WAR)—The income to the firm based upon the hours billed. Assuming your billing rate is $500 per hour and you bill and collect 1,500 hours, your WAR is $750,000. While not necessarily a rule of thumb any longer, for someone who is not a producer, past practices have pegged compensation by a rule of threes: one-third to overhead, one-third to profits, and one-third to salary. In the example, compensation of $750,000 in WAR would be $250,000. Such formulas are rarely used today, but they give you an idea and rough estimate of what your compensation is likely to be, plus or minus the impact of other factors. Non-discretionary bonuses are often paid if your WAR exceeds a particular threshold, e.g., $1 million. There can be discretionary bonuses paid on top of that as well. Understand your firm's compensation package and work it.

- Realization—The percentage of the hours you bill to the revenue earned. For example, if you billed 1,500 hours but collected on 1,200 of them, your realization would be 80% (1,200/1,500=.8). This is often compared to the firm's overall realization to see where you fit in the overall profitability. Realization can be measured at both the attorney and client level. At the client level, it reveals write-offs and can often reveal unprofitable clients. So, when you manage a client relationship, it's important to track both your and the client's realization. Last, if you oversee the billings to a client, pay particular attention to realization. Remember that every hour written off will negatively impact your realization, so don't be quick to write off time. All too often, attorneys write off time before it is billed and then write off more when a client complains about a bill. That's getting hit twice. The better approach is to bill 100% and then react if a client objects with an appropriate write-off. Don't assume a client will object before you bill a matter. In all my years of practice, I have never lost a client overbilling, and I rarely, if ever, wrote off time before it was billed. Trust in the integrity of your colleagues and bill all their time.

- Profitability—A calculation that considers various factors to determine a particular client's profitability. This is sophisticated and not used by many firms. In its simplest form, the more hours devoted by attorneys with lower billing rates, the more profitable the client is. Likewise, the larger the team that works on a matter, the more profitable it's likely to be. That may sound anti-intuitive until you realize that lower billing rates are assigned to more junior and more profitable attorneys. This is why delegating work to attorneys with lower billing rates is always a good idea when managing a matter.

- Utilization—The percentage of hours you bill to the target you're given. For example, if your billable hour target is 1,800 hours and you bill 1,700 hours, your utilization is 94.4% (1,700/1,800=.944).

Appendix E

What this should measure is whether you're busy enough and meet targets. When your utilization exceeds 100%, people notice and conclude that you are more profitable. Being above 100% can also mean you are overworked or do not delegate enough work. Thus, high utilization is a two-edged sword.

- Originations—The income from clients you originate. The higher the number, the more impact you have on the firm's financial performance. In its purest sense, attorneys with high originations are sometimes called rainmakers, but there is more to originations than income from clients you bring into the firm. It also relates to the income you bring in on the matters you manage where you are not the originating attorney. So, when you look at your originations, it's a combination of the total fees earned by the clients you originate (by all attorneys who work on the client) and the fees earned on matters you work on for clients you did not originate. Here's an example of how it works:

Client	Income
Income on a client you originated from all attorneys	$1,400,000
Income on your collected hours for Clients you did not originate	$700,000
Total	$2,150,000

In this example, you are responsible, directly and indirectly, for $2,150,000 of firm income.

All these numbers matter, and you can track them with precision. As you see one of them dropping, you can adjust your approach and try to remedy the problem. Likewise, when you see them working well or where you're exceeding firm averages for realization and utilization, you can think more about delegating work and building your book.

Of the two, the one most influential on rising to the top tier in a firm is the total fees received on clients you originated. That makes sense. There are just so many hours you can personally bill and collect. However, there is virtually no income limit on hours billed and collected by other attorneys you delegate work to. The ultimate prize is won on total revenue from clients you bring into the firm. So don't do all the work yourself. Delegate.

One last point on originations. As you grow in a firm, other lawyers will either leave or retire, and someone else has to take responsibility for the overall client relationship. That person will receive the benefits of those originations as well. Taking over a client, saving one from leaving the firm with a departing attorney, or inheriting control from a retiring attorney are all important ways to increase your origination credits that lead to promotion and higher compensation.

Ask your accounting department or your executive assistant to give you monthly reports on your numbers. Track them closely and react where appropriate.

Appendix F

Maintaining Your Reputation

Like it or not, promotion and compensation are often more about who you know than who you are or who knows you. You need a specific plan to build your reputation and be sure you're on the radar of the people who make the decisions. You can hope that will happen by chance or simply because you do good work, but that is a risk you do not have to take.

Below are some pointers that will help build your reputation. Many seem obvious. The question, however, is whether you execute on any of them or have excuses not to do so. Weak excuses include, "I'm too busy," or "I'm not comfortable speaking," or "I need to focus on billable hours." The bottom line is that if you don't find the time and overcome your fears, you will likely be passed over for promotion. Ask yourself, "Do my excuses justify my being a worker, or do I want to be a leader?"

- Speaking Engagements. When given the opportunity, accept speaking engagements. They may be a conference where you can speak or a meeting within the firm itself. Volunteer to present CLE to your colleagues. Promote it on your firm's website and social media accounts when you speak.

- Scholarship. Write firm bulletins and blogs. Use programs like Passle to show your expertise. If you are ambitious, consider writing white papers or books on your area of expertise.

- Pro-Bono. Volunteer and make sure those in management are aware of your pro-bono activities. It shows that you pay it forward above and beyond your day-to-day responsibilities.

- Self-Promotion. If you have an excellent result in a matter or win a case, get it posted on the firm's internal website. Where appropriate, announce it on social media sites like LinkedIn. It's OK to brag a bit because if you don't, no one will. That said, don't be shy in asking others to post your wins as well. One caution: check with the ethics rules in your jurisdiction on publicly naming clients or using any endorsements. Rules on lawyer advertising differ substantially from state to state.

- Ratings. There are seemingly countless rating organizations. Some are pursued by firms, e.g., Chambers and Legal 500. Others you need to pursue yourself, e.g., Super Lawyers, Best Lawyers in America, etc. While I do not believe they're responsible in any significant way to attracting clients, they get you ink and allow you, where states allow it, to include it in your email signatures.

Most importantly, you need to have the *conversation*. It can be awkward, and you may feel you're becoming a pest, reminding people of your goals. Doesn't everyone have the goal to advance in the firm's hierarchy? Then why bug your superiors by reminding them you are in the mix of the masses who hope to be promoted? Hopefully, the phrasing of that question provides you with the answer. If you view yourself as part of the masses, you will be treated as such and easily overlooked.

This is not rocket science. All you're trying to do is ensure the decision-makers know who you are and what you want.

When you have a conversation—in person, on the phone, via email, or via Zoom—make sure you also ask the person what more you can do to succeed. Make them your patron, or at least listen to their suggestions. They need to know you respect their opinions and will act on them.

- "Thanks for including me in the Zoom meeting. As you know, I'll be up for promotion soon and hope I'm doing everything I can to be considered. Is there anything more I should do?"
- "I know promotion season is coming soon and that I may be under consideration. Is there anything I should do to best present my case?
- "I just wanted to drop you a line to let you know the significant results we achieved for [client] in the [name] matter. Working with the entire team was a pleasure, and I'm pleased we got such an

Appendix F

    excellent result."

- "Thank you for including me on the [name] matter. It's the work I want to do as I make my career here. Let me know if I can help with more cases and what more I can do to gain needed experience."

If you have a good relationship with a client for whom you got an excellent result, ask them to send you or your immediate superior an email congratulating you on the result. Maybe you'll be lucky to even get an unsolicited email praising your efforts. Either way, such emails are worth their weight in gold. When you get one, share it with your immediate superior, who can then share it with other decision-makers.

None of this is hard. You just have to remember to do it. Here's one way:

Appendix G

Promotion Bingo

One of the best tactics to ensure promotion is to ensure you're recognized by the people who count and contribute to the promotion process. You know who they are, but do you have a plan to make sure they know who you are, what you've done, and that you want to be promoted? Do you have a plan to "sell" yourself to the decision-makers? Here's a simple suggestion: write down all their names and create a record of when you've had contact with them in person, by email, by phone, via Zoom, etc. The grid below, dubbed Promotion Bingo, is an example.

The first vertical column includes the names of all the people who you need to ensure know who you are. The balance of the vertical columns provides spaces for an entry each time you interact with them. Each box should have one "event." Over time, the grids will fill in, and you'll be assured you're recognized. You can do it in other ways if this grid isn't to your liking. Doing something in writing forces you to remember to meet those who chart your future. If you don't, no one will.

Person	What? Date	What? Date	What? Date	What? Date	What? Date	What? Date	What? Date
John Doe							
Jane Doe							
John Smith							
Jane Smith							
Etc.							

Appendix F

It could not be made simpler. The question is whether you do it, despite how trivial you may think the exercise is. Don't let your ego impede fundamentals.

Appendix H

Transition Program Ideas

While some law firms have programs to address senior lawyers, most do not, particularly mid-sized to smaller firms. Where they do, they primarily focus on reduced hours and vague references to mentoring. When you are thinking about options in forming a plan for yourself or your firm, here are some ideas to consider:

1. Phased Retirement Programs: Offer phased retirement options where senior lawyers gradually reduce their workload over a period leading up to retirement, e.g., reduced hours, responsibilities, or client workload.

2. Mentorship and Knowledge Transfer Programs: Create mentorship programs where retiring senior lawyers can pass on their knowledge and experience to junior lawyers or successors, preserving institutional knowledge and fostering professional development.

3. Flexible Work Arrangements: Provide flexible work arrangements for senior lawyers nearing retirement, such as telecommuting options, part-time schedules, or job-sharing arrangements, allowing them to maintain a work-life balance while transitioning into retirement.

4. Financial Planning and Retirement Benefits: Offer financial planning resources and retirement benefits to help senior lawyers prepare for retirement, including help with pension plans, 401(k) options, and other retirement savings vehicles.

5. Continuing Education and Professional Development: Support ongoing professional development opportunities for senior lawyers to stay updated with legal trends and advancements in their practice areas, even as they approach retirement.

Appendix H

6.   Retirement Celebrations and Recognition: Organize retirement celebrations and recognition events to honor the contributions and achievements of senior lawyers as they transition into retirement, including farewell gatherings, testimonials, personalized tokens of appreciation, or an annual acknowledgment at a firmwide meeting. Establish professional recognition awards or honors to acknowledge the contributions and achievements of retired senior lawyers within the firm and the broader legal community, celebrating their legacy and impact. If there are organizations that recognize the contributions a lawyer has made, nominate them for consideration.

7.   Alumni Networks and Connections: Maintain alumni networks or connections to stay in touch with retired lawyers and provide opportunities for continued involvement or collaboration with the firm on a voluntary basis. Create online alumni engagement platforms or networking forums where retired senior lawyers can connect, share experiences, and stay informed about firm news, events, and professional opportunities. Hold meetings where retired lawyers discuss the challenges and solutions in their transitions.

8.   Client Transition Assistance: Provide support and resources for senior lawyers to transition their client relationships smoothly with other attorneys within the firm, facilitating introductions, coordinating client meetings, and ensuring effective communication throughout the transition process.

9.   Sabbatical or Extended Leave Options: Offer sabbatical or extended leave options for senior lawyers nearing retirement who may wish to take time off before officially retiring, allowing them to pursue personal interests, travel, or spend time with family while maintaining a connection to the firm.

10.   Legacy Projects: Encourage and compensate senior lawyers for undertaking legacy projects or initiatives that contribute to the firm's long-term success or benefit the legal community, including writing articles or books, participating in pro bono work, or mentoring aspiring lawyers.

11. Health and Wellness Programs: Implement health and wellness programs to support the physical and mental well-being of senior lawyers, including access to healthcare resources, counseling services, and wellness activities. Host retirement planning workshops or seminars to educate senior lawyers about various aspects of retirement planning, including financial planning, estate planning, and lifestyle considerations. Provide retirement lifestyle coaching services to help retired senior lawyers navigate the psychological, social, and economic aspects of retirement planning, including adjustments to leisure activities, social networks, and personal goals. Invite experts to provide guidance and answer questions.

12. Post-Retirement Consulting Opportunities: Create opportunities for retired senior lawyers to continue working with the firm on a consulting basis, providing expertise and advice on specific projects or cases as needed, allowing them to stay engaged in the legal profession while enjoying more flexibility in their schedules. For example, consider establishing a panel of senior lawyers available for quick, off-the-cuff advice on something that might concern a client. Make that available only within the firm or by direct contact with clients.

13. Social and Networking Events: Organize social and networking events for retired senior lawyers to stay connected with colleagues and peers within the legal community, including alumni reunions, professional association gatherings, industry conferences, or annual firm meetings.

14. Transition Support Services: Offer transition support services to help senior lawyers navigate the logistical and emotional aspects of retirement, such as help with healthcare enrollment, relocation services, or access to retirement counseling resources. Add transition workshops and seminars specifically tailored to the needs and concerns of senior lawyers approaching retirement, covering topics such as emotional readiness, social adjustment, and identity transition beyond the legal profession.

15. Legal Aid Clinics: Partner with legal aid organizations or establish firm-sponsored legal aid clinics where retired senior lawyers can volunteer

Appendix H

their time and expertise to provide legal help to low-income individuals or marginalized communities.

16. Elder Law Services: Offer specialized elder law services for retired senior lawyers to assist elderly clients with estate planning, guardianship matters, healthcare directives, and other legal issues relevant to aging populations.

17. Entrepreneurial Opportunities: Support retired senior lawyers who wish to explore entrepreneurial ventures or start their own legal consulting businesses by providing mentorship, resources, and networking opportunities within the firm's ecosystem.

18. Professional Development Grants: Establish professional development grants or stipends for retired senior lawyers to pursue further education, certifications, or specialized training in areas of personal or professional interest beyond traditional legal practice.

19. Corporate Board Placements: Facilitate corporate board placements or advisory roles for retired senior lawyers seeking opportunities to leverage their legal expertise and leadership experience in corporate governance and strategic decision-making capacities.

20. Legal Research and Writing Projects: Offer legal research and writing projects or assignments to retired senior lawyers who enjoy scholarly pursuits and wish to continue contributing their analytical skills and legal insights to academic publications or legal journals.

Appendix I

Recommended Reading

Throughout the book, I've recommended various books that might be helpful to readers. I've read many business development and retirement planning books, including some targeted at lawyers. Most are lacking because the authors never had individual practices to build or transition, nor the experience of being in the trenches. Here are some relatively recent ones I found worth reading. Each has nuggets that will give readers good ideas:

Business Development for Lawyers, Sally J. Schmidt (2006).

Business Development: A Practical Handbook for Lawyers, International Bar Association, Stephen Revell, Consulting Editor (2016).

Best Practices in Law Firm Business Development and Marketing, Deborah B. Farone (2019).

Retirement by Design, Ida O. Abbott (2020).

Rainmaker Roadmap, Kimberly A. Rice (2021)

Designing a Succession Plan for Your Law Practice, Tome Lenfestey and Camille Stell (2021).

Four Thousand Weeks: Time Management for Mortals, Oliver Burkeman (2021).

How to Know a Person, David Brooks (2023).

Acknowledgments

I dedicated this book to my many mentors throughout my life and career. I would have never achieved the measure of success I've enjoyed without them. While I'll undoubtedly miss many, a few impacted my life more than most. My wife for never telling me I was crazy in my many ventures, but who at the same time kept me grounded when I got too close to the edge. My mother for her ever-present, upbeat personality and for teaching me to look on the bright side of life even in the worst of times. My father for reminding me not to ignore the darker side of people. Bob Viles for teaching me how to think like a lawyer. Bob Rines for inspiring me to be an entrepreneur and to see risk as a positive force, not a negative obstacle. Eddie Phillips for giving me invaluable business advice on measuring business success and knowing when it was time to let go. Felix Kent for the opportunity to become an advertising lawyer and who taught me the business of advertising as much as he did the law. Sam Friedman for showing me the importance of compassion in running a business. And many others. I encourage readers to list their mentors and what they taught you. It's a cathartic exercise worth the investment.

I'd also like to thank Nancy Schulein, my EA for over twenty-five years, Carol Bernstein, a special person in the life of one of my closest, now passed, friends, and Jeremy Townsend for their collective editing, helping make this book better. And, of course, thanks to Mitch Becker, my friend since grade school, for his thoughts. He's been a pre-reader on every one of my books. Thanks to my buddy, Arnie Lawner, for his insight. And thanks to my publisher, Plum Bay Publishing and its leader, Claire McKinney, for their continued faith in my writing. Without my team, this book would have never been possible.

If you're interested in personal coaching, let me know. I offer one-on-one sessions and ongoing coaching. I can be reached at douglas.wood@wood.law.